Design History

In 1922 all the major naval powers signed up to the Washington Treaty, an agreement designed to stop the kind of competitive naval building programs that had preceded the First World War. This treaty limited the number of battleships and total naval tonnage that each country could build, but it also defined the upper limits of tonnage and armament for each major warship type. For cruisers maximum gun size was 8in and displacement was not to exceed 10,000 tons. Having just signed a treaty intended to halt naval competition, all of the signatories then set about building to the maximum limits. With the building of battleships forbidden for ten years the focus was on cruisers. The naval race was on again, with 10,000-ton 8in gun cruisers as the new measure of naval supremacy.

Paradoxically, in most navies the cruiser function was better suited to smaller ships with quick-firing 6in guns that could be built more cheaply and in greater quantities. The 8in cruiser, later called a Heavy Cruiser (as opposed to the 6in gunned Light Cruisers), was therefore created as a result of treaty restrictions rather than actual need. In fact, only the US and Japan had any real need for large cruisers – because of the long distances involved in the Pacific theatre. A large cruiser could carry the extra fuel needed for greater range.

Initially the United States built ten treaty cruisers to a similar concept: 10,000 tons,

600ft long, nine or ten 8in guns, 5in/25cal secondary armament, 32 knots speed, but lightly armoured and not well protected. These types generally matched what the other navies were building but because of their flimsy protection they were not ideal ships. By the 1930s the initial excitement of building what came to be called 'Treaty cruisers' had calmed down. With the exception of the United States and Japan other countries started building the more useful 6in types for scouting and screening duties. The United States and Japan, however, continued building heavy cruisers and a 'second generation' of this type was embarked upon. The *New Orleans* class was the first of this second generation of Treaty cruisers. They formed a bridge between the original ten and the sophisticated war-built *Baltimore* class. They were slightly shorter than their predecessors but more robust. They were much more heavily armoured and the armour was distributed more effectively.

The General Board of Naval Construction wanted a more resilient type of heavy cruiser. Five ships had already been authorised by Congress and two of them were already under construction to a modified first generation design. The other three were not started until a very different design was ready. This design was shorter, with the required thicker armour and improved scheme of protection. This more compact arrangement was made at the sacrifice of the unit principle of propulsion. The unit

A view of the *Astoria* before the war. One can see the purposeful lines, the stacks forward and the large well-deck behind them that distinguished this class from its predecessors.

principle (used in previous and subsequent classes) grouped a set of boilers with a turbine room and another set of boilers with another turbine room. The idea was that a single hit should not disable the ship's entire propulsion system by destroying either all of the boilers or the turbines. The *New Orleans* class had all of the boilers forward, which enabled a closer grouping of the stacks (and more room aft for aircraft handling) and the turbines in one large area under the hangars. This meant that a single lucky hit could indeed disable the ship's propulsion system – but this sacrifice was made so that a shorter but much thicker armour belt could be included.

■ DESIGN CHARACTERISTICS

Compare the 8in turret on the *Tuscaloosa* (left) with that of the previous classes – in this case the *Chicago*. Also note the ship number atop turret No 3.

Dimensions	Length, oa 588ft, wl 578ft; beam 61ft 9in; draft 22ft 8in; height above water – bow 29ft, stern 16ft, bridge 77ft, stack 75ft, mast 116ft
Displacement	10,047 tons standard, 13,719 tons full load (1944)
Propulsion	8 Babcock and Wilcox boilers, Parsons geared turbines
Power, speed	107,000shp, 32.75 knots
Endurance	7600 nm @ 15 knots
Armament	Nine 8in (3 x 3), eight 5in/25 cal (8 x 1), eight .50cal (8 x 1)

The *New Orleans* design was heavily influenced by the 'gun lobby', an influential group of admirals who felt that gunfire was the ultimate weapon and that emphasis on surface gunnery would be the decider in battle situations. Weapons such as torpedoes, mines and aerial bombs were secondary in importance. The gun lobby also believed that any likely opponents were similarly minded and that future conflict would be decided by ships of like type slugging it out using their main armament as the arbiter. As a result the *New Orleans* class were better protected against medium-calibre gunfire at the expense of protection against mines and plunging projectiles such as bombs and very long range gunfire. They were expected to get

■ 8-INCH 55-CALIBRE GUN MARK 12

Length	37ft 5in
Weight	17.5 tons
Muzzle velocity	2800f/s
Maximum elevation	41°
Maximum range	31,700yds
Rate of fire	2.1rpm
Projectile weight	260lb

close to enemy heavy cruisers and survive.

Their armament reflected this: nine 8in guns mounted in a well armoured turret rather than the lightly protected gunhouses of the previous classes. These turrets allowed individual elevation of each gun and, although smaller, were so arranged for more rapid fire. The secondary armament of eight 5in/25cal remained the same as the previous classes but it was located forward and had superior fire control. The 5in/25 was a dual-purpose weapon – used for surface action and against aircraft. True to the tenets of the gunnery lobby this was the first class of Treaty cruisers designed without torpedo tubes. Previous classes had included torpedo tubes in their design although they were later removed. Initially there were also eight .50-calibre machine guns for AA purposes, but as time went on the AA armament was increased considerably. The 50cal machine guns were too light and were replaced by 20mm Oerlikon machine cannons; 1.1in quads were added

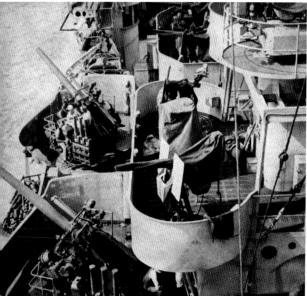

Left: A view of the *San Francisco*'s portside 5in/25cal secondary armament. Note the large opening in the breech for fast loading.

Below: A view of the forward turrets of the *New Orleans* in 1944. This turret design was found on the first three members of this class – with a rounded turret face and slightly larger gun barrels.

Above: Even with a spacious well-deck the demand for space encroached upon the aircraft-handling area. The aircraft were often stowed on the catapults.

Below: The aircraft-handling cranes were situated atop the hangar which was used for stowage of the ship's boats. These cranes also doubled as boat cranes.

in 1940 and then replaced by the more effective 40mm Bofors weapon.

The Mk 12 55-calibre 8in gun was a formidable weapon capable of firing a 260lb projectile a distance of 31,700 yards (nearly 18 miles). These guns could fire at a rate of slightly over two rounds a minute; this rather slow rate of fire was to be a limitation in fast-moving night actions. These guns were mounted in a more compact turret which was lighter and better armoured that the ones used in the previous classes. The last five units of this class had a slightly improved turret with a flat face and slightly less weighty guns spaced slightly further apart in the turret face. This turret design was the basis for all future triple 8in gun turrets.

These guns were guided by one 12ft rangefinder mounted on the top of the bridge on the fire control platform and two Mk 33 gun directors mounted just behind the rangefinder forward and atop the aft fire control position on the hangar.

The secondary armament of 5in/25cal dual-purpose guns was similar to previous classes. The relative shortness of the barrel sacrificed accuracy and range in return for ease of handling and rapidity of fire (a trained crew could fire 14 rounds a minute). It could be elevated up to 85 degrees and fire a 54lb shell as high as 27,000ft.

SCOUT PLANES

The *New Orleans* class were possibly the best-equipped cruisers in the US Navy for handling scout planes. These aircraft were vital to the cruiser's primary mission of scouting and needed to be kept in good condition in an onboard hangar. The *New Orleans* class had a capacious hangar that could accommodate four seaplanes abaft the stacks and just forward of the aft 8in turret. This positioning of the hangar was different from the preceding classes, where it had been amidships athwart the aft stack. The new layout provided more room and there was a large well-deck forward of the hangar for ease of aircraft handling. The catapults were raised on pillars on each side of the well-deck and above the hangar were two aircraft-handling cranes (a newer model

CHANGES TO ANTI-AIRCRAFT ARMAMENT

	.50cal	20mm	1.1in	40mm
1940	8	–		
1941	12	–	16 (4 x 4)	
1942	–	12	16 (4 x 4)	
1943	–	12-20	–	24 (6 x 4)
1944	–	20-26	–	24 (6 x 4)
1945	–	8-28	–	26 (6 x 4, 1 x 2)

The *Astoria* launches her SOC Seagull spotting plane.

with a control compartment), one for each catapult. This arrangement made aircraft handling quicker and easier as well as giving increased space for aircraft stowage.

With the exception of the *Alaska* class CB the *New Orleans* class was the last cruiser class to have the hangar and catapults located amidships. All subsequent classes had the hangar below-decks aft and the catapults on the stern.

This cruiser class was the newest and best at the start of the war. As such it was in the front line – particularly after the disaster at Pearl Harbor decimated the US battlefleet, when the absence of capital ships made heavy cruisers, in effect, substitute battleships. The *New Orleans* class had to perform as battleships more than once during the war.

The *New Orleans* at the start of hostilities. These cruisers had to spearhead the offensive against Japan; they had the fighting qualities needed to succeed.

Careers

I t would be difficult to identify any warship class that had a more distinguished war record in the history of the US Navy. The *San Francisco* and *Minneapolis* received 17 battlestars (more than any other cruiser) and the *New Orleans* received 16. The *San Francisco* also received the Presidential Unit Commendation.

In the mid-1930s the *New Orleans* class were the newest and most prestigious cruisers in the US Navy. As such they were often used on diplomatic missions and had flagship status on fleet exercises, making even their peacetime careers noteworthy. In 1939 the Japanese Ambassador to the United States, Hiroshi Saito, died in Washington. At that time relations between Japan and the United States were strained so President Roosevelt decided to make a gesture of friendship. He chose one of the newest and most prestigious ships in the navy, the *Astoria*, to deliver the ashes of the Ambassador to Japan. This succeeded in repairing relations and the brand new cruiser and its crew and captain Richmond Kelly Turner were welcomed and entertained lavishly in Yokohama. The next time the *Astoria* encountered the Japanese the welcome was very different.

OPENING ROUNDS

At the time of Pearl Harbor the *Quincy* and *Tuscaloosa* were in the Atlantic, the *Vincennes* and *Astoria* were at sea escorting carrier groups who were delivering planes to Wake Island, the *Minneapolis* was 20 miles south of Pearl conducting training exercises, and the *San Francisco* and *New Orleans* were in Pearl Harbor itself when the attack came. The *New Orleans* was lightly damaged by a fragmentation bomb, which wounded a score of sailors, but none were killed. Such was the confusion and inexperience of American pilots that the *Minneapolis* was incorrectly identified as a Japanese aircraft carrier. The *Minneapolis* compounded the problem by miscoding a message to Pearl Harbor, sending the message 'Two carriers in sight' instead of 'No carriers in sight'. Fortunately, the US aircraft sent after these two carriers recognised the *Minneapolis* and halted their attack.

With the US Navy battlefleet effectively eliminated, the heavy cruiser acquired the new role of big-gun substitute alongside the traditional missions of escorting carrier groups and scouting. As the newest and best of their type the *New Orleans* class were to become heavily engaged.

The *Vincennes* escorted the *Hornet* and *Enterprise* on their daring raid on Tokyo, and the *New Orleans* and *Minneapolis* escorted the *Lexington* and *Yorktown* for their strike on Rabaul. The *Minneapolis*, *Astoria* and *New Orleans* were all present at the Battle of the Coral Sea, screening the aircraft carriers *Lexington* and *Yorktown*, a role that they would assume more and more as the war progressed. When the *Lexington* was hit, the commander of the US task force, Rear Admiral Fletcher, transferred his

The last ship of the class to complete, *Vincennes* is seen passing through the Panama Canal on 6 January 1938 en route to a fleet exercise in the Pacific, less than a year after commissioning. The ship later returned to the Atlantic but was back in the Pacific by the time of the Pearl Harbor attack.

command to the *Astoria* and continued the battle from her. The *Lexington* was sunk and the *Yorktown* was damaged but the Japanese invasion force bound for Port Moresby was turned back.

After Coral Sea the *Astoria*, *Minneapolis* and *New Orleans* hastened back to Pearl Harbor with the damaged *Yorktown*. At Pearl they were joined by the *Vincennes*, freshly back from the raid on Tokyo with the carriers *Hornet* and *Enterprise*. The damaged *Yorktown* was repaired in four days flat and set out with her two sister carriers to confront the might of the Japanese navy. These four cruisers, along with four others, formed the screen for Task Forces 16 and 17.

The Battle of Midway was a carrier battle where opposing surface forces never sighted each other. The three US carriers surprised the Japanese and sank all four of their fleet carriers at the cost of the *Yorktown*. Without carrier cover the rest of the Japanese fleet had to turn back from its objective, Midway Island. The cruisers performed valuable duties such as AA support, rescuing downed airmen and lending assistance to the damaged *Yorktown*. Again Admiral Fletcher had to transfer his flag to the *Astoria* when the *Yorktown* was hit.

This battle was the turning point in the war in the Pacific. The US Navy now went on the offensive, with the *New Orleans* class cruisers spearheading the surface forces.

GUADALCANAL 1942

Battle of Savo Island, 8/9 August. Six of the seven members of this class were assembled in the South Pacific for the operation to capture Guadalcanal. Only the *Tuscaloosa* – still in the Atlantic – was missing. This is where the class was blooded and acquired its reputation: by the end of this campaign all six were either sunk or out of action. This was a high casualty rate but these ships were essential to the success of what became a crucial campaign.

This force of cruisers was split amongst those accompanying the invasion force (the *Astoria*, *Quincy* and *Vincennes*) and those escorting the carriers in support (*San Francisco*, *Minneapolis* and *New Orleans*). On 26 July 1942 groups of transports, escorts, and carrier task forces from Pearl Harbor, San Diego, Tonga, Samoa, and New Caledonia rendezvoused off the Fiji Islands. This was the largest concentration of US naval power since the attack on Pearl Harbor, and six of the seven *New Orleans* class cruisers were present at this occasion.

The *Quincy* opened the Guadalcanal campaign with salvos from her nine 8in guns, bombarding Japanese positions on Guadalcanal and provided anti-aircraft cover for the transports when they were attacked by Japanese torpedo bombers on 7 and 8 August. The presence of torpedo bombers prompted Admiral Fletcher, who

was in charge of the carrier force, to withdraw prematurely, so the invasion force was left without air cover.

To protect the transport from a night surface attack Admiral Victor Crutchley, in charge of the transport screen, separated his available cruisers into three forces. The two weakest cruisers were to guard the eastern entrance of Sealark channel – the least likely direction of attack. The six available heavy cruisers were stationed in two groups at the western entrance of the Sealark channel. The heavy units of the northern force were made up solely of *New Orleans* class cruisers – *Quincy*, *Astoria* and *Vincennes*.

An attack was not expected – even though a Japanese force was spotted heading in the direction of Guadalcanal earlier that day. The ships of all three forces were patrolling as though it was a routine peacetime exercise. The flagship, HMAS *Australia*, had even detached herself to take the force commander, Victor Crutchley, to a conference onboard one of the transports.

A view of the burning carrier *Lexington* at the Battle of the Coral Sea taken from the deck of the *Minneapolis*.

The *Astoria* recovers one of her scout planes in the Pacific. In order to do this the cruiser would turn in an arc around the plane to create a flatter surface on the water in the ship's lee.

The forces were not on full combat alert; unfortunately the Japanese were. The Japanese force, consisting of five heavy cruisers, two light cruisers and one destroyer, slipped past the advanced scouting patrol of two destroyers and hit the southern force hard, and within ten minutes it was destroyed as an effective fighting force. Only one ship – the destroyer *Patterson* – had even radioed an alarm. The ships of the northern force, ten miles away, observed the action to the south and were wondering what to make of the *Patterson*'s message 'warning warning strange ships entering the harbour'.

Gunichi Mikawa, the Japanese Admiral, was informed that there were ships to the north and he turned north – *away from the transports* – to confront this new menace.

During this turn northward his force had split into two columns and it was between these two columns that the *Quincy*, *Astoria* and *Vincennes* were caught. Even though the *Patterson*'s warning and the battle to the south was observed by the bridge personnel on all three cruisers, they were not ready for the onslaught. Captain Greenman of the *Astoria* was not even on the bridge and Captain Moore of the *Quincy* was also just arriving. Unprepared, their armament not fully manned and ready, caught in glare of searchlights, the three cruisers were sitting ducks for the Japanese force.

Within half an hour three *New Orleans* class cruisers were fatally damaged by a Japanese force of a similar size – not a good performance for ships that were supposed to incorporate the highest standard of protection and fighting qualities. However, the result was not so much an indication of poor design as it was of battle unreadiness, disorganised damage control, and poor practice – especially in having fully-fuelled floatplanes on the catapults during battle. The highly flammable aviation fuel not only caused massive damage when ignited but it also illuminated each ship as a target. When the lessons of this battle were learned, the remaining members of this class were to able to absorb far greater damage and yet remain afloat.

Survivors of the *Quincy*, *Astoria* and *Vincennes* could take some small consolation from the fact that by turning to confront the northern force Mikawa was deflected from his primary objective – the transports sitting off Lunga Point. The loss of the transport fleet would have meant the end of the Guadalcanal invasion and the probable stranding of the 1st Marine Division. So in this sad way these cruisers ultimately contributed to the success of the Guadalcanal campaign.

There were now only three *New Orleans* class cruisers in the South Pacific, and within two weeks they were in combat

Astoria discharges her main armament on the way to Guadalcanal.

providing screening and anti-aircraft support for the carriers *Wasp* and *Saratoga*. A week later the *Wasp* was sunk by a submarine and its screen, including the *San Francisco*, was dispersed amongst various other task forces. So it was on 13 October that *San Francisco* became the flagship of Task Force 64, a surface action group assembled to block a reinforcement group screened by three Japanese heavy cruisers heading for Guadalcanal.

The Battle of Cape Esperance, 11/12 October. TF64 was commanded by Rear Admiral Norman Scott, an intelligent and able officer who had a clear plan as to how to fight a night surface battle. His novel idea was to organise his mixed force in a single line ahead for ease of control (this proved successful and was later adopted, with great effect, in the Battle of Surigao Strait). He put a division of three modern destroyers in the van and a couple of extra DDs in the rear, with his four cruisers in the centre – the flagship *San Francisco*, *Salt Lake City* and the large light cruisers *Boise* and *Helena*. These ships had been exercising night manoeuvres for the previous three weeks under Admiral Scott's command, specifically to increase their readiness for a night battle.

This force arrived off the western approaches of Ironbottom Sound just before midnight. The *San Francisco* was the only one to successfully launch a scout plane and this was aloft for the entire battle. Scott's force commenced patrolling, waiting for the Japanese. On their first counter-march the force turned south using a manoeuvre that had been practiced many times but in light of what happened next was unwise. The counter-march consisted of the van destroyers swinging out wider than following cruisers speeding along the flank of the column and then

joining the van again when the cruisers were passed. Unfortunately, this was done just as the heretofore unseen enemy force came into range, putting the van destroyers, *Farenholt*, *Laffey* and *Duncan*, between the US and Japanese cruisers.

The US cruisers had orders to open fire as soon as they had the enemy is their sights and not to wait for orders. The *Helena* and *Salt Lake City* saw the oncoming Japanese cruisers and let loose as fast as they could fire. The Japanese were caught completely by surprise, heading into a maelstrom of gunfire and only able to use their forward weapons. Admiral Scott had performed the classic manoeuvre of crossing the enemy's T, but Scott was still worried about the van destroyers, missing somewhere between his cruisers and the enemy. He ordered his ships to cease firing and personally ensured that his flagship, the *San Francisco*, complied with his order. After locating the *Farenholt*, he allowed his ships to resume fire but four minutes were lost and this allowed the surprised Japanese to strike back. They landed some 8in hits on the *Boise*'s forward magazine, killing every man in them, and the ship was nearly sunk by a magazine explosion. Fortunately, the magazines were flooded through the holes caused by the original damage. The *Duncan*, one of the van destroyers, had turned towards the Japanese force to make a solo attack and was caught in the crossfire between the two opposing forces. The *Duncan* was hit many times by both US and Japanese shells and was disabled and out of the battle fairly early on.

After the firing resumed and the American line became disordered, it turned into a confused action. Admiral Scott was aware that he was hitting his own ships as well as the enemy's and ordered a withdrawal. Still, the American force got the

The *New Orleans* and *Astoria* on manouevres off Fiji on the way to invade Guadalcanal. Note the floatplane landing behind the *New Orleans*.

Below: A weary and battered *San Francisco* arrives in port after the Battle of Guadalcanal. Some splinter damage can be seen on her bridge wing – and these can still be seen at her monument in San Francisco where her old bridge remains to this day.

Above: The hangar door was shredded by splinters. When the *San Francisco* emerged from the dockyard after an extensive refit and repair she had a different type of hangar door – one that folded to the side rather than rolled up.

better of the engagement by sinking the cruiser *Furutaka*, destroyer *Fubuki* and severely damaging the Japanese flagship *Aoba* for the loss of the *Duncan* and damage to the *Boise*. The flagship *San Francisco* distinguished herself in the first of two battles that were to earn her the Presidential Unit Citation.

The Battle of Guadalcanal, 13 November.
This battle was the turning point of the Guadalcanal campaign. For four months the United States and her allies had contested the island with the Japanese. Even though there was almost daily land combat and four major naval battles had been fought, neither side had gained the advantage. By early November both sides were gearing up for one last major push. The US sent two convoys of seven transports from Noumea escorted by five cruisers and eleven destroyers. The *San Francisco* was flagship of the escorting forces carrying the flag of Rear Admiral Callaghan. The Japanese prepared a convoy of eleven transports in Bougainville, which was to be preceded by a bombardment force of two fast battleships, a cruiser and eleven destroyers to knock out the US airfield on Guadalcanal – Henderson Field – so that the Japanese transports could approach unmolested by air attacks.

The US reinforcements arrived first, defended by the cruisers against air attacks from Japanese bases in Rabaul 600 miles to the north. The *San Francisco* was hit in her after control station, severely wounding her executive officer, Commander Crouter. Despite his injuries he elected to stay with his ship for the ensuing night battle. Bad choice.

The US had to protect Henderson Field at all costs, so the cruiser force escorting the reinforcement convoys were ordered to stop the more powerful Japanese bombardment force from carrying out its mission, whatever the consequences. Admiral Callaghan led his cruiser force out of Ironbottom Sound with the now empty transports creating the impression of leaving the sound vacant for the Japanese to bombard Henderson Field without opposition. Then, under the cover of darkness, Callaghan detached eight destroyers and his five cruisers – *Atlanta*, his flagship *San Francisco*, *Portland*, *Helena* and *Juneau* – and headed back into Ironbottom Sound to confront the oncoming Japanese bombardment force.

The Japanese force suspected nothing – they thought that they would have an uncontested run at the airfield. Callaghan was new to his job – this was his first combat assignment as an admiral in charge – and his Flag Captain, Cassin Young, had just joined the *San Francisco* five days before. Callaghan had formulated no battle plan nor did he communicate with any of his captains what his intentions were. He just formed a cumbersome line ahead formation of four van destroyers, five cruisers (in the order given above), and four

destroyers bringing up the rear, and sailed into Ironbottom Sound. Soon there were reports of contact with the enemy: first by radar, then visual contact. The Japanese had also sighted the US ships but were not sure of their nationality. Callaghan's task force was not allowed to open fire – they had sailed into the centre of the Japanese formation at very close range. Finally the battleship *Hiei* turned her searchlights on the unmistakeable profile of the cruiser *Atlanta* and all hell broke loose.

Belatedly Callaghan radioed the order to his force: 'Odd ships commence fire to starboard even ships fire to port'. This was confusing, as his ships were not sure whether they were even or odd and often they were tracking targets on the wrong side. The engagement quickly degenerated into a melee with ships firing away at anything and at very close range. The *San Francisco* took the battleship *Hiei* under fire and then switched to the *Atlanta*. As soon as Callaghan realised what was happening he ordered 'cease firing own ships'. This was most likely meant only for the *San Francisco* but the message went out over radio to the whole task force, creating more confusion. Fortunately, the Japanese were as confused as the Americans as the battle deteriorated even further.

Shortly afterward the bridge of the *San Francisco* was hit by a 14in shell that killed Admiral Callaghan and all but one of his staff, and mortally wounded Captain Young. Any hope of bringing order to the US task force ended with that and the ships all fought individual battles with each other and the Japanese. The battle degenerated into total chaos; it was, as one historian put it, 'like minnows swimming in a bucket – Japanese ships intermingling with US ships'.

The *San Francisco*'s top command was wiped out: the admiral, captain, exec, first lieutenant and navigation officer were all dead or mortally wounded. The *San Francisco* was engaging two Japanese battleships at close range. There were over 45 shell hits and 25 fires were raging over the ship. Command devolved to two lieutenant-commanders, Bruce McCandless, the signals officer, and Herbert Schonland, acting first lieutenant. McCandless conned the ship while Schonland in overall command attended to damage control. These two junior officers fought the ship through the Japanese task force whilst putting out fires and leading the other surviving US ships out of danger. For this they were each awarded the Congressional Medal of Honor.

With the *San Francisco* retiring and the *Hiei* immobilised by numerous hits, the battle wound down, leaving six US ships heading back to Noumea, two cripples unable to move out of Ironbottom Sound and five others sinking or sunk by the Japanese. The badly damaged and immobile *Hiei* was sunk later that day, joining

A close-up view of the battering that the *San Francisco*'s superstructure took. The holes on the starboard bridge wing were caused by the 14in shells which killed Admiral Callaghan, his staff and Captain Young.

two Japanese destroyers that had been sunk the night before.

Despite all that went wrong, the US forces prevailed that night. They stopped the bombardment force and inflicted as much or more damage on a superior force than they suffered from the Japanese. Quite possibly it was the confusion; US sailors proved better able to cope with the chaotic situation that ensued when the two forces became hopelessly entangled.

The Battle of Tassafaronga, 30 November /1 December. The last major surface battle in Guadalcanal waters involved the two remaining *New Orleans* cruisers in the Pacific. They were lucky to survive.

This battle came about when the Japanese were desperately trying to supply their starving troops by sneaking in small, fast destroyer task forces at night. These destroyers were laden with supplies and replacement troops, which impaired their fighting ability, but they were able to slip in under cover of darkness, deposit their cargo and get out before daylight brought on air attacks.

On 30 November the US forces tried to surprise and intercept one of these Japanese task forces. Under Rear Admiral Carlton Wright a powerful force of five cruisers – the *New Orleans*, *Minneapolis*, *Pensacola*, *Northampton* and light cruiser *Honolulu* – accompanied by six destroyers was sent to stop a Japanese force of eight destroyers, six of them laden with troops and supplies. To ensure that the floatplanes on the US cruisers were not a liability they

were sent to Tulagi before the battle and the gasoline lines drained so as to not be a fire risk. A battle plan was drawn up – the destroyers were to attack first with torpedoes and then the cruisers would open fire on the ships that survived.

The powerful cruiser task force crept into Ironbottom Sound and detected the oncoming Japanese ships on their radar. The lead destroyers requested permission to fire torpedoes; belatedly the answer came back – affirmative. Unfortunately, the targets had passed and the torpedoes had to chase the Japanese destroyers at a poor target angle. Then the five cruisers opened up, but they all went for the lead Japanese destroyer, the *Takanami*. They scored hit after hit and disabled the *Takanami* within minutes after opening fire. The Japanese were completely surprised but they reacted resolutely and skilfully. This was a result of excellent night training and the leadership

The *New Orleans* a month after Tassafaronga. The curvature of the face of Number 2 turret is clearly visible after the Japanese kindly removed 180ft of the bow to allow a closer inspection.

U.S.S. NEW ORLEANS 3 JANUARY, 1943
From forward at Frame 36

of Rear Admiral Tanaka, one of the best combat admirals of the war. Without firing a shot (which would have revealed their location) the remaining destroyers put over twenty torpedoes in the water, turned close to shore to decrease visibility, and got away as fast as they could, heaving provisions overboard for the soldiers ashore to retrieve as best they could.

Within five minutes the torpedoes struck. First was the *Minneapolis*, hit by two torpedoes in the bow and losing the entire bow section forward of Number 1 turret. The *New Orleans*, behind the *Minneapolis*, swerved to avoid the damaged *Minneapolis* and was hit in the forward magazine – its whole bow was also blown off, right up to Number 2 turret. So sudden was this that an observer on the stern of the *New Orleans* saw the bow floating past with its turret pointing to the sky and reported that the ship had just passed the sinking *Minneapolis*. The *Pensacola* was next: a torpedo smacked into her aft engine room and set off a fire that shot as high as the mainmast. Last was the *Northampton*, hit by two torpedoes and sunk as a result. The Japanese destroyers had defeated a much more powerful force for the loss of only one destroyer. Post-battle analyses confirmed the following reasons for the loss:

- the rate of 8in gunfire was too slow to hit fast moving targets at night,
- night training is all-important,
- and the efficacy of the Japanese torpedo tactics was at last recognised.

There were now three very badly damaged *New Orleans* class cruisers in South Pacific waters. They all made their way painfully back to Pearl Harbor and thence to the West Coast shipyards for repair and rebuilding.

With a temporary bow the *New Orleans* slowly makes her way back to the USA where she will be refitted with a new bow, turret and superstructure. The new turret will have a rounded face just like the others.

The *Minneapolis* and *New Orleans* had lost their bows and had to have temporary ones built out of coconut logs at Tulagi just to get them to Noumea.

REPAIRS AND REFITS

Within four months of the start of the Guadalcanal campaign all six cruisers of this class in the Pacific were either sunk or out of action. The Japanese cruiser force was similarly decimated, with the entire *Kako* class out of action and half the *Mogami* class also sunk or out of action. There was a hiatus on both sides as they repaired their damaged ships. The three surviving *New Orleans* cruisers active in the Pacific, *New Orleans*, *San Francisco* and *Minneapolis*, were extensively modified during their long stay in drydock. Anti-aircraft defence was now a priority as their new role was seen as support for the fast fleet carriers. The bridges were rebuilt to a narrower profile to eliminate topweight and give the AA guns a wider firing arc. New radar and electronics were also installed.

Not only were damaged ships repaired during the relatively quiet year of 1943 but the Pacific Fleet commissioned 5 new fleet carriers, 5 light carriers, 14 new cruisers and 73 new destroyers. The Japanese could not keep up: they were only able to commission 3 light cruisers and 10 destroyers in the same period.

In October 1943 the 'Big Blue Fleet' (Task Force 58) debouched from Pearl Harbor as part of 'Operation Galvanic', the reconquest of the Gilbert Islands. This comprised 6 fleet carriers, 5 light carriers, 6 new fast battleships, 8 cruisers and 44 destroyers. The Pacific War was transformed and the desperate battles of the Solomons were a thing of the past.

The fast carrier task forces dominated the Pacific from late 1943 onwards and the surviving cruisers were part of these task forces, providing AA support and surface screening. These forces could stay at sea for months on end as there were able to refuel and re-store at sea by tankers and freighters specifically designed for underway replenishment.

The *San Francisco*, *Minneapolis* and *New Orleans* were all present at the Battle of the Philippine Sea, the largest carrier battle in the war where fifteen US carriers engaged nine Japanese carriers. The US carriers were trying to protect the transports that were attacking Saipan, and the Japanese were trying to disrupt the landings. The Japanese had the advantage of longer ranged airplanes and mobility; however, their air groups were not what they once were. The US aviators outclassed them and outnumbered them – 430 of the Japanese attackers were shot down by AA fire or combat air patrols. The losses on the US side were 10 percent of that. It was called the 'Great Marianas Turkey Shoot' by those involved, and the *New Orleans* cruisers did their fair share of turkey shooting.

The role of the cruiser had changed over the course of the war from scouting and surface engagement to shore bombardment and screening the fast carrier forces. It is fitting, however, that in the last major battle that *New Orleans* class cruisers engaged in their traditional roles of scouts and attacking surface forces.

THE BATTLE OF LEYTE GULF

The greatest naval battle in history was the battle of Leyte Gulf. This was actually a series of related engagements between the IJN and the USN and its allies. In a desperate last gamble the IJN sent its entire remaining fleet against the forces invading the Philippines. The most potent striking force was the nine remaining Japanese battleships, two of which, the *Yamato* and *Musashi*, were the most powerful in the world. The IJN's renowned carrier strike force was a shadow of its former self, having lost almost all of its experienced aviators in previous battles. On paper they still had a respectable carrier force but in reality it was weak because of the lack of experienced pilots.

The Allied forces greatly outnumbered the Japanese navy at this stage of the war, but any invasion force is vulnerable when landing troops and immobile. The invasion force was protected by the powerful Third Fleet under Admiral Halsey with six modern battleships and seven aircraft carriers. The essence of the Japanese strategy was to use its powerful looking but impotent carrier force to lure the Third Fleet north while the surface forces struck at the invasion shipping. To further confound the Allies the IJN split its surface strike force into two task forces – a more powerful northern strike force, which included the *Yamato* and *Musashi*, and the weaker southern force to act as a pincer attack on the invading fleet.

The battle was fought as a series of skirmishes and four major engagements. The first engagement was when the northern strike force was attacked by aircraft of the Third Fleet. The *Musashi* was sunk but the rest of the fleet was relatively unscathed. This attack delayed the progress of the northern force for eight hours and convinced Admiral Halsey that the northern force was neutralised.

Tuscaloosa showing an unusually vibrant splotch pattern.

San Francisco bombarding enemy positions on Okinawa.

The next engagement was a surface action in Surigao Strait between the southern strike force and Allied surface forces assigned to screen the invasion force, The *Minneapolis* was one of the cruisers in this force. Anticipating an attack via the Surigao Strait by the southern force, the commander of the screen placed his more than ample forces carefully across the northern exit to the strait. Across the centre there were six old but rebuilt battleships; on the right flank there was a force of three cruisers; and on the left flank another five cruisers, including the *Minneapolis*. Down the strait were a couple of destroyer squadrons to scout and soften up the enemy. Against this well positioned force steamed a Japanese force of two battleships, an aircraft-cruiser and four destroyers.

In the early morning of 25 October 1944 the southern force was sighted by one of the destroyer squadrons. The destroyers executed a brilliant series of torpedo attacks that took much of the southern force out of the action. The remaining three ships (battleship *Yamashiro*, cruiser *Mogami* and destroyer *Shigure*) sailed into one of the most appalling situations a squadron could encounter – directly into the largest concentration of gunfire ever directed at a naval force. The *Minneapolis* was at the forefront and she and her consorts added materially to the weight of fire on the doomed *Yamashiro*. Within ten minutes the firing stopped: the *Yamashiro* was sinking, the *Mogami* ablaze, but the lucky *Shigure* was escaping, virtually undamaged.

Admiral Ohlendorff ordered the left flank cruisers down the strait to chase the cripples. The *Minneapolis* and her consorts engaged the burning *Mogami* and sank the crippled *Asagumo* before they were summoned back to Leyte Gulf to face a possible new threat from the northern force.

While the *Minneapolis* was engaged south of Leyte Gulf, the *New Orleans* was chasing Ozawa's decoy carrier force with Admiral Halsey and most of the Third Fleet.

Halsey's aircraft had damaged or sunk all the carriers and the remnant was fleeing north back to Japan. Halsey was racing to engage what was left of this force when he received urgent requests from the Seventh Fleet guarding the invasion shipping to confront the northern Japanese force threatening Leyte Gulf. With his prey nearly in sight Halsey turned his battleships and much of his screen around to head south to try to engage the *Yamato* and her consorts. However Halsey did not abandon his chase completely, sending Rear Admiral DuBose with the *New Orleans*, *Wichita* and two light cruisers ahead to destroy cripples.

In the late afternoon this force sighted the *Chiyoda*, listing and on fire. The *New Orleans* opened fire and disposed of the last carrier. They then chased further north and caught the *Hatsuzuki*, a fast modern destroyer which had come back to rescue any survivors; instead it found four US cruisers and a squadron of destroyers.

The *Hatsuzuki* put up a tremendous fight but was overwhelmed by the superior firepower of the *New Orleans* and her consorts. Thus ended the largest naval battle ever fought with the *New Orleans* and *Minneapolis* chasing down and destroying stragglers.

The rest of the war saw the remaining cruisers of this class revert to their roles as carrier escort and shore bombardment ships. They were joined at Okinawa by the *Tuscaloosa*, which up to then had enjoyed a solid but uneventful career in the Atlantic. There they bombarded the entrenched Japanese troops and fought off kamikaze attacks. Fortunately none of the *New Orleans* class ships were badly damaged during this campaign.

After the war the *New Orleans*, *Minneapolis*, *San Francisco* and *Tuscaloosa* were involved in repatriating US troops, and were then laid up. The most decorated cruisers of the US Navy were all stricken and scrapped in 1959; none was preserved for posterity.

Model Products

Although the *New Orleans* class were well known and attractive subjects, model kits of members of this class were not available until the 1990s. This is surprising because of the large number of lesser-known subjects that were available well before that. However, since then kit manufacturers have been making up for lost time and at present there are at least twenty-one different kits from six different manufacturers commercially available.

■ NEW ORLEANS CLASS KITS

Scale	Company	Kit	Comments
1/350	Trumpeter	San Francisco	1942 configuration
1/350	Trumpeter	San Francisco	Late-war configuration
1/350	Yankee MW	Quincy	Resin kit originally from Classic Warships
1/350	Yankee MW	San Francisco	Resin kit originally from Classic Warships
1/350	Yankee MW	New Orleans	Resin kit originally from Classic Warships
1/700	Waveline	San Francisco	1942 configuration
1/700	Waveline	New Orleans	1942 configuration
1/700	Yankee MW	San Francisco	Late-war – based on LCP kit
1/700	Loose Cannon	Quincy	Resin kit – OOP
1/700	Loose Cannon	Vincennes	Resin kit – OOP
1/700	Navalworks	San Francisco	Resin kit – OOP
1/700	WSW	Quincy	Resin kit

Scale	Company	Kit	Comments
1/700	Kombrig	Minneapolis	1944
1/700	Kombrig	Astoria	1942
1/700	Niko	San Francisco	1942
1/700	Trumpeter	New Orleans	1942
1/700	Trumpeter	Astoria	1942
1/700	Trumpeter	San Francisco	1942
1/700	Trumpeter	San Francisco	1944
1/700	Trumpeter	Minneapolis	1942
1/700	Trumpeter	Tuscaloosa	Not specified
1/700	Trumpeter	Quincy	1942
1/700	Trumpeter	Vincennes	1942

1/350 Scale

TRUMPETER *SAN FRANCISCO* 1942 — 1/350 Scale

As the first plastic kit of the most decorated cruiser in the US Navy, this kit caused great excitement when first released. Why it took until 2007 to appear is a mystery: remember the *Missouri* with only three battle stars appeared in plastic over fifty years earlier. The kit is very good – worth waiting for.

The hull is excellent: the dimensions measure out almost exactly, and the shape and sheer lines are captured accurately. This is the key to any ship kit, as the hull is the hardest to modify if there are any errors. There is a single row of scuttles (portholes) – correct for 1942. The scuttles are to scale and each one has an 'eyebrow' above it. The stem is very accurate – just the slightest curve in the gently raked stem.

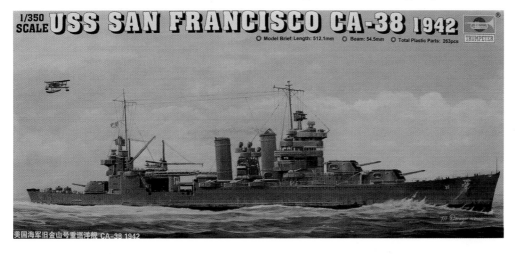

The first plastic kit of this class: the *San Francisco* steams into action, in box art by Mike Donegan, who did the box art for all but one of the Trumpeter *New Orleans* class kits.

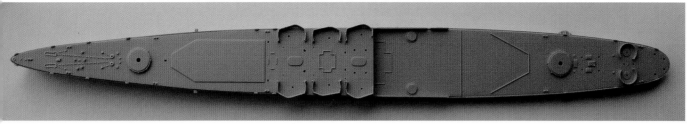

The splinter shields around the 5in secondary armament have been done with great attention to detail and accuracy.

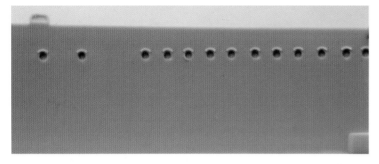

Each porthole or scuttle has a rigol (eyebrow) above it. This was correct throughout the war, even after some scuttles were plated over.

The supports for the yardarm can be seen here. They were much thinner on the foremast and were not on the mainmast at all. The searchlight tower lattice is done in plastic and is almost to scale – which is difficult to achieve in plastic.

On the minus side, the bow is a bit narrow around the No 1 turret and the hawsehole surround does not protrude from the hull as it should.

The deck is also of a high standard. The planking is just about to scale and is suitably lightly delineated, as planking should be. There is not much surface detail, since the kit is so designed that much of it is added later. This makes it easier to paint but requires more assembly work.

The weapons and small parts are not to the same high standard as the hull. The 5in guns are not well done in this scale as they are too low, lacking in detail and what detail there is, is incorrect. The Mk 33 gun directors are poor: they are far too small and inaccurate to boot. There are no after-

market parts and as this is a prominent feature the model builder may wish to scratch-build this complicated part. On the other hand, the 1.1in quads are nicely done, as are the ship's boats – especially the large ones. The 8in turrets and guns are also good, with realistic-looking blast bags attached at the base of the gun barrels. This means that the guns can only be set at one elevation, but this is the price one must pay for moulded-on blast bags.

Bulwarks and splinter shields tend to be significantly thicker at the base and this is hard to fix. However, there is good surface detail and the superstructure is quite accurate for *San Francisco* in 1942.

The masts have the yardarms moulded on and the yardarms seem to sprout directly out of the sides of the mast rather than a separate part attached behind the mast. There are supports for the yardarm on both the foremast and mainmast, but in the case of the latter this is inaccurate. In fact there were thin supports for the foremast yard, but the ones in the kit are too thick.

In summary this kit can be built up into a very good model, the basics are accurate and well done. It would benefit greatly from aftermarket sets and PE (photo-etch).

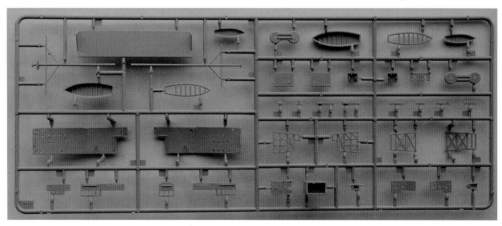

TRUMPETER *SAN FRANCISCO* 1944   1/350 Scale

This is pretty much the same kit as the previous one, with the addition of two different sprues to provide parts for the bridge and hangar and weapons.

The top of the hangar deck has moulded-on bulwarks – these should be replaced by railings. Also, the hangar door is incorrect. After the damage suffered at the Battle of Guadalcanal the hangar doors were replaced by a concertina-style door that was folded to the sides of the opening. Again Trumpeter got the major parts right

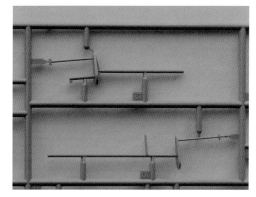

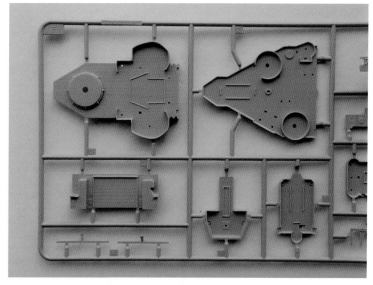

but there are some problems with the smaller parts. The masts, however, are nicer than those in the '42 kit. They are moulded with the platform and topmast in place, but the dimensions and angles are correct.

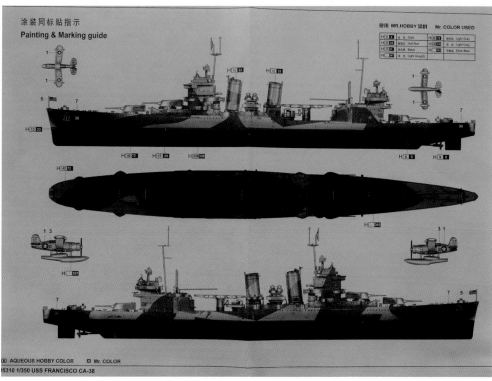

Above: There were no bulwarks between the 40mm gun tub and the aft control position; they should be removed from the model. Also the hangar door is correct for 1942 but was replaced by a different one in 1943.

Above, left: The masts and platforms are moulded in one piece, but the complex angles between mast, platform and topmast are all correct and the detail is crisp.

The kit comes with a painting guide, but unfortunately the camouflage scheme supplied only superficially resembles Ms 33/13d.

1/350 Resin Kits

Prior to the release of the Trumpeter 1/350 plastic kits Classic Warships made a series of *New Orleans* class resin kits in 1/350 scale. Classic Warships sold its kit business to Yankee Modelworks, which produces these kits now.

YANKEE MODELWORKS *QUINCY*   1/350 Scale

The *Quincy* is an accurate kit and the only one available in this scale. It was first produced over fifteen years ago and although it was state of the art at that time it has fallen behind the latest resin casting techniques. In particular the splinter shields and deck detail are rather heavy. There are white metal small parts for boats, weapons etc, which are nice, but one would want to replace some of them with the latest aftermarket parts cast in resin. Supplied

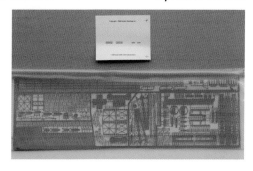

The PE is extensive and well detailed for the time it was first made but it is not relief etched.

The hull measures out exactly for length, beam and turret spacing. It is solid resin and cut to the waterline; there is no full hull option.

with the kit is a large photo-etch fret, which includes searchlight tower, catapults, yardarm detail, ladders, cranes and railings.

The master was made by Steve Wiper, who is known for his attention to accuracy, and with the addition of some extra photo-etch and aftermarket parts it will build up into a fine model – as evidenced by Ken Summa's model in this book.

YANKEE MODELWORKS
SAN FRANCISCO, NEW ORLEANS
1/350 Scale

■ The comments for the *Quincy* apply equally to these two kits. Again, the *New Orleans* is the only 1/350 kit available on the market, although it would be easier to modify one of the Trumpeter plastic kits to represent *New Orleans* than to turn it into the significantly different *Quincy*. When these three ships were first marketed the intention was to produce kits from which any ship of the class could be constructed.

1/700 Scale

There are three resin kits that are of such an outstanding quality that they should be considered before the excellent plastic products from Trumpeter.

NIKO *SAN FRANCISCO* 1942
1/700 Scale

The kit comes beautifully backed with plenty of parts and photo-etch. The small parts are so good there is no need for any aftermarket parts.

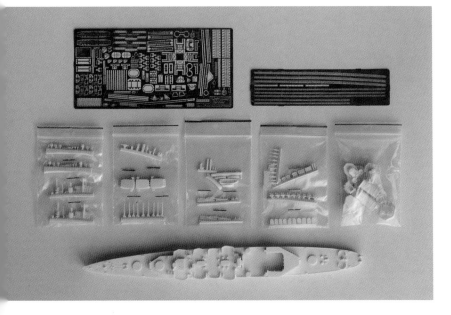

■ This is a beautifully cast, highly detailed and intelligently designed kit. Upon first inspection of the hull one sees a complex, intricate part with wafer-thin splinter shields, a hangar with the interior beautifully detailed, excellent deck detail and at least two levels of superstructure. It is surprising then, after this magnificent effort, to find some dimensional faults. The hull is 5mm too short, although the beam is correct. The stem is not correct either – it should be much straighter. This will be very difficult to correct although it will also be difficult to detect as well.

It comes with a photo-etch set that includes lots of ship-specific details, such as boat cradles, stack grills, detailed searchlight tower, platform supports, the specialised boat-handling davit, and crane attached to the catapult tower, and railings cut to fit (and with the correct curvature for the bow section). The masts are also provided in PE, which has the potential to give an excellent level of detail but may not be strong enough to support much rigging. It will also require careful painting and assembly to give it the rounded look that a mast should have.

The unique aircraft-handling cranes are largely done in photo-etch, with the control

This is a dramatic and complex casting which, unfortunately, is 5mm too short.

compartment at the base of the crane created by bending the PE around a rod. This will look very nice if done properly, but may be difficult to achieve for the average modeller.

This is an outstanding kit, but with some surprising dimensional shortcomings; and the innovative uses of photo-etch may present difficulties for a less skilled modeller.

KOMBRIG *ASTORIA* 1942   1/700 Scale

■ This is a Russian company whose name is often transliterated as Combrig. The *Astoria* is a finely cast and accurate model of the ship as she appeared in 1942. It comes with two frets of PE.

This is a waterline kit and the hull is cast without much surface detail, but the deck planking is very well done – it is the closest to scale of any of the kits on the market.

The hull is reasonably accurate though it measures out 2mm too short and 1mm too narrow. There is also a touch of tumble-home amidships which should not be there. This is solvable with a bit of sanding.

The superstructure parts are cast on to thin wafers and look easy to remove – as they should be, because they have extremely fine deck platforms attached to many of the superstructure parts. Things such as the splinter shields for the secondary armament are also cast on to wafers (which explains the lack of surface detail on the hull – these details are meant

to be added which can give a crisper finish to the completed model). The hangar can be depicted as open or closed; the walls are detailed inside as well as outside.

The 1.1in quad AA mounts are a wonder. This is the most delicate and intricate casting this author has ever seen. They are cast on resin blocks for ease of handling and removal; this is very necessary because the fineness of detail makes these parts extremely delicate. The same is true of the other accessory parts – they are all very detailed but fragile.

The box art features a picture of the *Astoria* at the beginning of the war.

The small parts of this kit are all of this quality.

The parts are well cast and very fine and delicate. Unfortunately, many of them are just lumped together in a ziplock bag and are susceptible to damage while shipping or unpacking.

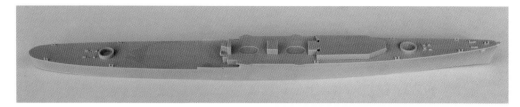

Compared to the Niko kit the hull looks positively bare. This kit has the same level and fineness of detail that the Niko kit has – it's just that the parts are added to the hull by the modeller rather than being already moulded on.

The two photo-etch sprues provide the searchlight tower, catapults, aircraft-handling cranes, radars, ladders and supports. There is a fret common to the *Minneapolis* and *New Orleans* kits and one specifically for the *Astoria*. The *Astoria* one contains the plating and windows of the signal bridge as well as the correct number of 20mm for this ship. The 20mm PE is an interesting configuration of shields and trunnion training wheel and the barrel with sight, ammo and shoulder rests. Unfortunately they are slightly overscale.

There is no railing in the PE, but it can be sourced elsewhere anyway.

With so many delicate parts, more attention could have been paid to packaging. Although the 1.1in quads were separately bagged, many other equally fragile parts were all in together and susceptible to damage while shipping or handling by the modeller.

Overall this kit is accurate and well cast. There are minor errors in the hull size and some of the PE sizes but it will build into a first-class *Astoria*.

Below: The bottom fret is common to both Kombrig kits, but the top one is specific to the *Minneapolis*.

Below, right: This is a correct and beautifully made director.

KOMBRIG *MINNEAPOLIS* 1944   1/700 Scale

The *Minneapolis* has much in common with the *Astoria* kit, such as the hull, many of the small parts and the hangar assembly, but as it represents a late-war appearance, there are some significant differences.

This kit is the only one on the market for *Minneapolis* at this time. It is configured as she appeared in 1944 in the Battle of Surigao Strait. As such it is very accurate and as well cast as the *Astoria* kit – indeed, the hull is the same; just add different parts and you have a *Minneapolis*. However, the splinter shields are cast separately and correct for a late-war *Minneapolis*.

Like the *Astoria* kit the small parts are

particularly well cast; in this case the 40mm quads are exquisite. There is some PE for the back rail. Each kit has two PE frets, one common to both kits and a kit-specific one.

The superstructure is accurate: the *Minneapolis* differed from her sisters in the late-war configuration in that the rebuilt bridge structure was a bit narrower fore and aft than the others. There were also differences in the position of platforms and this is all accurately and finely depicted. One complaint is that the large bridge windows that are unique to the *Minneapolis* just after her refit (and visible on the box top photograph) are not depicted on the model.

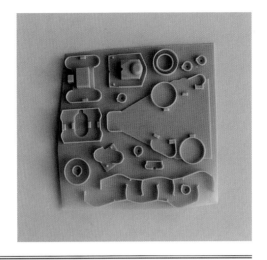

These parts are extremely fine and cast on a thin resin wafer, so care must be taken while removing them.

TRUMPETER *NEW ORLEANS* CLASS   1/700 Scale

■ When the kit of the 1942 *San Francisco* was released in 2008, it marked the beginning of an eight-kit program of *New Orleans* class cruisers in 1/700 scale. There are now kits for all seven cruisers of this class and two for the famous *San Francisco* (as she appeared in 1942 and in 1944; all other subjects are depicted as in 1942). There are essentially four different kits, but common sprues exist for all of them, so it is useful to look at these shared aspects first.

The kit comes with a split upper hull and an optional underwater section, so it can therefore be built as either full hull or waterline. It measures out perfectly and the shape appears to be the most accurate of any of the 1/700 kits. The stem is correct and the knuckle under the stern is captured perfectly. The hull has two rows of

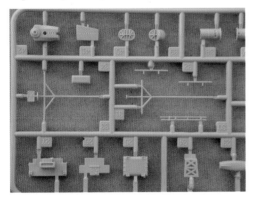

scuttles with 'eyebrows' moulded over the top row. The bottom row and some of the top would need to be filled in to replicate a wartime appearance; conversely, some more scuttles would have to be added to the bottom for a peacetime appearance. For detail and accuracy the hull is the best of any of the 1/700 kits available. The deck is also very nicely turned out, with finely scribed lines and very thin splinter shields.

Each kit comes with two weapons and accoutrements sprues. The 8in guns and turrets are well done, with the gun barrels to scale and a very realistic blast bag moulded on. There are two types of turrets – the one used for the *New Orleans*, *Astoria* and *Minneapolis* with a rounded turret face, and a flat-face turret for the rest. The cranes are also well done, although the lattice work would be better done in photo-etch. However, the Mk 33 gun directors are too small and incorrectly formed – the rangefinder should be at the front of the director. The 5in, 40mm and 20mm weapons are not very good, but the very

The sheerline of this class is captured very well in this kit. The 'eyebrows' over the portholes give the hull some texture.

Interestingly this is the only kit where Mike Donegan was not responsible for the box art. It is a very nice painting but there are some inaccuracies with the turret face and bridge windows.

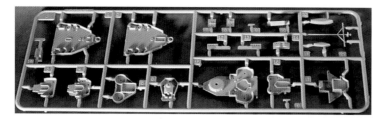

These parts are specifically for the unique *New Orleans* bridge configuration and can only be found in this kit.

small and fine detail parts are difficult to achieve in plastic, which is why many modellers prefer to use photo-etch or after-market resin parts. The rafts and searchlight are acceptable and small plastic ladders are included. This is preferable to the 'Aztec' steps found on so many plastic models but still not as good as photo-etch.

The 40ft boats are in two parts – hull and seats – and are very nice, while the 26ft whaleboats are satisfactory. The mainmasts for the early-war ships are not quite right. They have large supports for the yardarm when in fact there were none. The foremast has supports but they are overscale. The yardarm is not attached aft of the mast as it should be, but just sprouts off to the sides of the mast. This is common for most plastic kits, however.

So much for the sprues common to all kits, but Trumpeter has also made a serious effort to capture the minor differences between sister ships – for example, as already mentioned, there are the two types of turrets available on the weapons sprue.

New Orleans. This kit has the original set of sprues designated A-E. Sprue D is the one unique to this kit and it has the distinctive *New Orleans* bridge configuration with the signal bridge open and an expanded platform on the navigation bridge. Interestingly, the box art has this wrong: it

depicts a plated-in signal bridge. The hangar also has minor differences reflected in this sprue in that the 20mm gallery around the aft control position only has two Oerlikons. The searchlight tower is a plastic lattice rather than a monolithic plastic block as may be found on other plastic kits, but it is still a bit thick and would better be replaced by photo-etch. Overall this kit is a good representation with lots of attention to minor details.

Minneapolis, Astoria, San Francisco. These three ships are covered by the same kit. It appears to be designed to be accurate for the *San Francisco*, with the minor differences of the other two regarded as close enough to be ignored. In this kit sprue D is replaced by Sprues H and J. These have slightly different hangar decks with the *San Francisco*'s 20mm and boat positions and a 20mm gallery with four mounts. The bridge is correct, with the signal bridge level plated in and the windows a deck-and-a-half high.

The *Astoria* and *Minneapolis* use the rounded turret faces and the *San Francisco* has the flat-faced turrets. Again these kits will build up into good representations of their respective ships, with some minor scratch-building needed on the hangar deck for the *Astoria* and *Minneapolis*.

Tuscaloosa. After the manufacturer's attempts at capturing the subtle differences between the first four ships of this class, the *Tuscaloosa* kit was received and examined with great interest. Would it have the signal bridge plating at one deck level high? Would the fourth pair of 5in/25s be indented? Would the searchlight tower be mounted atop the vent rather than straddling it? – the disappointing answer was No. This kit is a departure from the accurate and well-researched kits in the rest of the Trumpeter 1/700 *New Orleans* class range. Instead, what was in the box were the parts necessary to build a *Quincy*. The distinctive features of the last two ships in the class, *Quincy* and *Vincennes*, were all there – exposed barbettes, joined splinter shields, smaller bridge structure. In reality, the *Tuscaloosa*

These bridge parts are correct for the *San Francisco*. Note the part with the windows for the signal bridge.

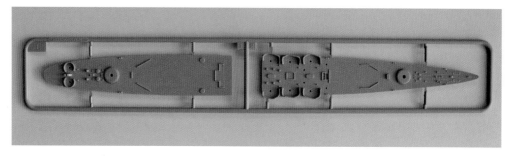

This piece is used in the first four kits of this series. The 5in splinter shields are correct, as is the turret spacing and anchor details.

was similar to the *San Francisco*, with the exception of the points mentioned above. None of the modifications intended for the *Quincy* are appropriate for the *Tuscaloosa*. About the only thing correct is the spacing between the first two turrets – which makes it incorrect for the *Quincy* and *Vincennes*.

Quincy and Vincennes. These kits contain the same sprues as for the *Tuscaloosa*, and as such the *Quincy* builds up into a fairly good replica, with the exception of the first

turret being too far forward. The turret in the kit is in the same place as in the previous kits, whereas in actuality the last two ships of this class had their forward turrets placed about 9ft aft so as to shorten the armour belt. There is a new deck sprue that has the different pattern of splinter shields that the *Quincy* had, but this is not accurate for the *Vincennes*, which had separate shields for each gun, much in the same manner as the *San Francisco*, *New Orleans*, et al. It is disheartening that after going through all of the

At least the box art matches the model.

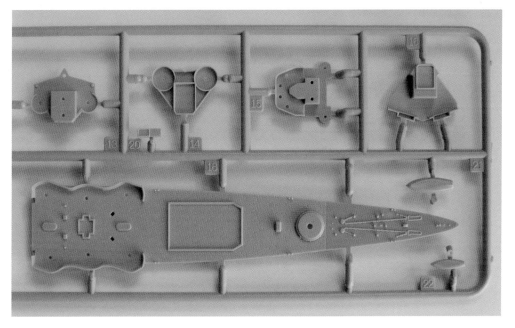

This sprue is found in the *Tuscaloosa*, *Quincy* and *Vincennes* kits. The bridge details are fine for the *Quincy* and *Vincennes* but incorrect for the *Tuscaloosa*. The foredeck has the correct splinter shield arrangement for the *Quincy* but is wrong for the others – which were each unique. The turret spacing is incorrect for the *Quincy* and *Vincennes* but correct for the *Tuscaloosa*.

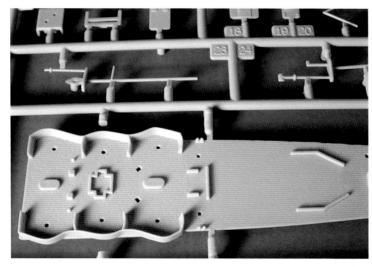

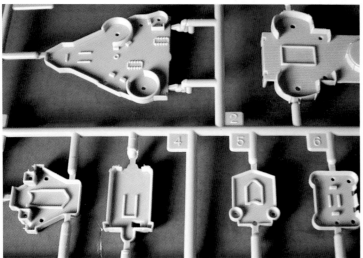

trouble of developing the new deck sprue that the turret was not placed further aft or the anchor capstans further forward as was correct for these two ships. Another issue is that the stacks are common with the other kits, whereas the stacks of the last two ships in this class were slightly smaller and more slender.

The *Vincennes* kit is accurate in that there is a separate part for the top of the bridge, replacing the 'bird bath' platform that the *Quincy* had up to her demise. The *Vincennes* had this feature removed before her splinter shields were fitted, and her bridge profile is distinctively different than the *Quincy*'s. The box art has this correct and can be used as a reference.

San Francisco 1944. The late-war *San Francisco* kit is similar to the 1/350 offering from Trumpeter, with the same strengths and weaknesses, although there are several exceptions: the masts which worked well in 1/350 do not translate well to 1/700. The moulding of the mast assembly with platform and topmast does not look convincing in this scale. Similarly, the smaller weapons such as the 40mm and 20mm are indistinct and overscale. They should be replaced by aftermarket parts.

Top: The decks on all of the Trumpeter kits are nicely done. The splinter shields are correct for a late-war *San Francisco*. Note the masts just above the deck on this sprue.

Above: This is part of a special sprue for the late-war version of the *San Francisco*. The top of the hangar part has a bulwark between the 40mm gun tub and the control tower than needs to be removed.

WSW *QUINCY*   1/700 Scale

■ This resin kit is still in production and is well cast and accurate. In particular, the bow turret is in the correct place and the anchor detail is more correct than the plastic equivalent. It is a very nice kit but does not have the something extra that the Niko and Kombrig kits have. It is a lot older and casting techniques have improved since then. Still, it will build into an accurate *Quincy*.

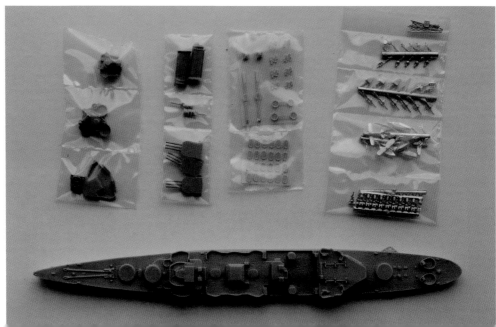

LOOSE CANNON PRODUCTIONS
QUINCY, VINCENNES

1/700 Scale

■ Loose Cannon Productions makes resin 1/700 ship model kits and specialises in esoteric subjects. These were some of the very first kits produced by the company – and they look it too: the casting is poor and requires a lot of clean-up, and some of the small parts are unusable. This has changed in their later offerings, but these two kits are now out of production. That said, the *Vincennes* kit is the most accurate representation ever produced in this scale, with correct splinter shields, smaller stacks and correct position of the No 1 turret. If one is prepared to spend the time cleaning either of these kits up and using aftermarket parts for the smaller armament, they build into a very nice model.

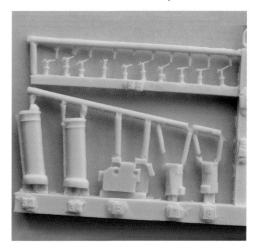

These stacks are slightly thinner – which is correct for these members of the class. Also note the quality of the casting; it can be cleaned up fairly easily, however.

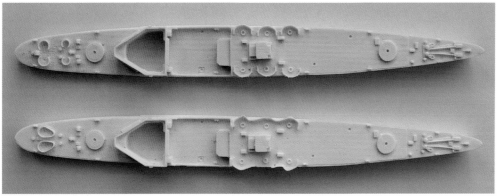

The LCP *Vincennes* (top) and *Quincy* hulls. Note the difference in the splinter shields for the 5in guns, and also the difference in the 1.1in gun tubs on the fantail. These are the most accurate of the kits in this respect.

WAVELINE *SAN FRANCISCO, NEW ORLEANS*

1/700 Scale

■ Waveline is a resin model kit manufacturer associated with Pit Road in Japan. These two kits were among the first kits of the *New Orleans* class to become available in the early 1990s. They were fine kits for their time but casting techniques have moved on since then and the newer models have more to offer. They also suffer from being 3 percent too small – apparently this is a result of the master being made exactly to scale and the shrinkage of the mould while cooling was not accounted for. With the exception of scale, the basics are very well done and with addition of aftermarket sets these can be built into very nice models.

NAVALWORKS *SAN FRANCISCO*

1/700 Scale

■ This kit has long been out of production but if one is already in the stash or obtained secondhand, it is worth building. It is correct in size and accurate, but the casting can be variable, depending on the batch. A good one will build up into a decent model, however.

Accessories

WHITE ENSIGN MODELS *NEW ORLEANS* CLASS PHOTO-ETCH SET
1/350 scale

■ Comprising two frets, this is a very detailed and complete set designed to enhance the Trumpeter 1/350 *San Francisco* kits. It contains photo-etch for all of

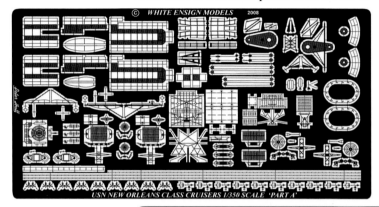

the things that the medium is suited for, such as cranes, stack grilles, radars, railings, searchlight tower, catapults, mast platforms and ladders, but it also includes components that are normally cast in resin or moulded in plastic. The 40mm quads are an example. They are made up of a number of components, some of them folded to give bulk and when assembled they provide a look of delicate detail that is surprisingly three-dimensional due to the folding and doubling. Nevertheless, the trunnions and gun barrels themselves still lack solidity if viewed closely. Some of these photo-etch components, such as the gun sights and platforms, could be used to enhance solid parts from either the kits or aftermarket sets.

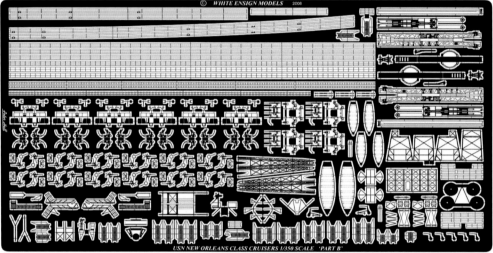

GOLD MEDAL MODELS *NEW ORLEANS* CLASS PHOTO-ETCH SET
1/350 scale

This is similar to the WEM set in much of the basics, but it does not have complete AA weapons – just detail parts. It does have life raft bottoms and rigging for the cranes.

■ **Contents:** custom-fitted railing for the main decks plus ample railing in several styles for all remaining decks and platforms; inclined and vertical ladders; radars; funnel cap grilles and detailed catwalks for both funnels; details for 40mm

Bofors guns, 20mm Oerlikon cannon; 5in/25cal gun mounts; 1.1in quad machine guns; bottoms for all life rafts; life raft paddles; correctly-detailed replacement yardarms for both masts; watertight doors in open and closed positions; cable reels in two sizes; correctly-detailed replacement searchlight platform; two detailed aircraft catapults; two crane booms and rigging; accommodation ladder with davit; rudders, pulpit rails, aft decks, and support cradles for ships' boats; struts and propellers for two SOC Seagull seaplanes; replacement 3-D relief-etched splinter shields for 5in/25cal gun mounts; assorted hand-wheels; two propeller guards; and a binnacle for the ship's bridge. Unlike the WEM set, it does not contain the complete Bofors or Oerlikon mounts – just details to enhance the kit or aftermarket items.

L'ARSENAL 5IN/25CAL GUNS   1/350 scale

Made in France by the USN admirer Jacques Druel, these are very nice replacements for the Trumpeter and Yankee Modelworks 5in guns included in their kits.

They are very detailed and accurate, and come with a photo-etch sprue for extra detailing. The 1/350 models featured in this book all use these.

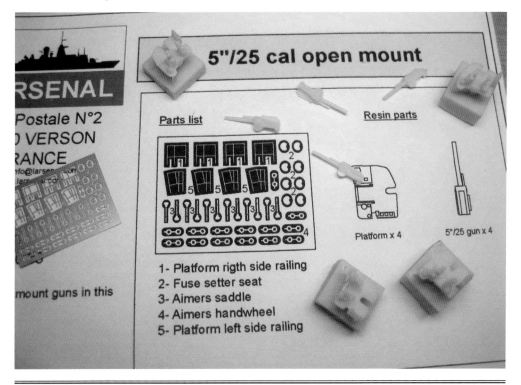

A general-purpose fret with lots of useful items for detailing a 1/700 *New Orleans* class cruiser. Of particular interest are the railings and details for the 5in/25s.

GOLD MEDAL MODELS
USN CRUISER/DESTROYER SET   1/700 scale

This is a generic set of details suitable for US cruisers and destroyers of World War II. It is an excellent set with lots of useful parts to detail one's *New Orleans* class kit, such as tiller and rudder for the whaleboats, radars, TBS antennae, bridge windows, yardarm details, railings, scout plane catapults, etc. It does not have the distinctive *New Orleans* class searchlight tower or aircraft-handling cranes. One may wish to combine this set with a more specific PE set such as the Tom's Modelworks *New Orleans* set or the White Ensign Models set listed below.

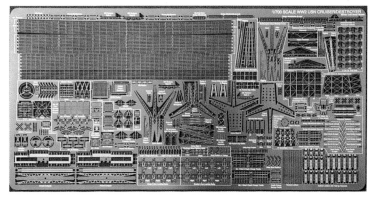

TOM'S MODELWORKS
US HEAVY CRUISER SET 717   1/700 scale

This set has what the GMM set lacks – namely the searchlight towers, and in two versions: one for the first five and a slightly smaller one for the *Quincy* and

Vincennes. Also, aircraft-handling cranes and a small assortment of ladders, scout plane struts, railings and radars.

WHITE ENSIGN MODELS *NEW ORLEANS* CLASS
PHOTO-ETCH SET   1/700 scale

This is a comprehensive set of photo-etch designed specifically for the 1/700 Trumpeter kits but useful on any 1/700 *New Orleans* class kit. It has just

about everything one needs: catapults, stack grilles, searchlight tower, 40mm quads, 1.1in quads, 20mm, seats and gunwales for the larger ship's boats, rail-

There are two types of searchlight towers – one that straddles the main vent between the stacks and another slightly smaller one for the *Quincy* and *Vincennes* which sits atop the vent.

This is an excellent set which has a wealth of items that can be used to detail a *New Orleans* class cruiser. The 1.1in quads are particularly nice, as are the yardarm details.

A more three-dimensional look is achieved by using thicker photo-etch and lots of folding.

This resin kit contains eight 5in/25cal bases and barrels and one base and breech for a practice loader.

Right: These have incredible detail for resin and are easy to assemble. The platform behind the guns is cast in resin but needs a railing behind it.

Below: Note the incredibly fine detail on the resin bases. It also comes with photo-etch, including platform, and instructions.

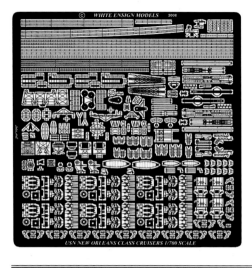

ings, aircraft handling cranes, and just about every type of radar fitted to these cruisers during World War II. The catapults in particular are a work of art with incredible detail. The 40mm quads are overscale, however, and even though there is doubling up of gun barrels some may find photo-etch a bit two-dimensional for these large and complex weapons. The 20mm are nicely done but they are so small and detailed that one will have to be very careful and highly skilled to get the best out of these. This set is well worth having.

VOYAGER 40MM QUAD BOFORS   1/700 scale

These guns are more to scale than the WEM 40mm but not quite as elaborate. They are less difficult to assemble but still suffer from the two-dimensional look.

They can be built up a bit with careful painting and they have a nice delicacy which is difficult to achieve with resin alone.

CORSAIR ARMADA 5IN/25CAL GUNS   1/700 scale

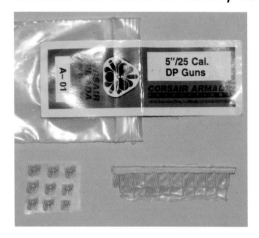

This set is designed to replace the inaccurate and badly detailed 5in/25cal weapons found on so many US cruiser kits. It is to scale and correct but has no PE for railings or other fine details. It would benefit from combination with the GMM Cruiser/Destroyer fret, which has the railings and other small details for 5in/25s.

LOOSE CANNON PRODUCTIONS
40MM QUAD BOFORS   1/700 scale

These are entirely made from resin and very detailed, accurate and in scale. They are not too hard to assemble but because they are so delicate they are susceptible to damage. However, the resin is not brittle, so careful handling is enough to avoid harm, although the softness of the resin can make the barrels curve. There is no photo-etch for railing or shields – these have to be added from aftermarket PE sets.

NIKO 40MM QUAD BOFORS   1/700 scale

These are also very detailed weapons and in scale. They come with PE platform, gunsights and railing. They are easy to assemble, although the barrels are stiffer than the LCP ones. This means that they

are straighter and easier to break. The photo-etch looks nice, but the back railing is not accurate. However, since these weapons are in gun tubs, it is impossible to see.

Modelmakers' Showcase

SCRATCH-BUILT *MINNEAPOLIS* 1/350 Scale By PIERRE MARCHAL

Pierre Marchal is an outstanding modeller who lives in Paris. He has been interested in warships and ship modelling ever since as a young boy – this was in the 1950s – he watched a lot of movies about the Pacific War. The naval battles around Guadalcanal, the Philippines and Pacific atolls captured his imagination and started a lifelong interest in the USN. With techniques taught to him in a high school woodwork class, Pierre used wood and the drawings from *Jane's Fighting Ships* to construct scratch-built models of his favourite US ships in 1/1530 scale (most of the drawings in *Jane's* were to this unusual scale). He taught himself other scratch-building methods so that he was not restricted to building whatever kits were available in the local hobby shop – he could build whatever he was interested in, and all in the same scale. Pierre has never built a plastic model.

His modelling activities lapsed during university studies, marriage and starting a career. Pierre worked in the petrochemical industry and has travelled extensively worldwide, ending up as the manager of a jewellery company based in Spain before he finally retired in 2007. During his career he never lost interest in ship modelling and at the age of 35 he stated again with a more satisfying scale of 1/500.

Below: Searchlights, whaleboat and secondary armament are all cast in resin.

Bottom: Pierre used rolled paper to make the 8in barrels. The turrets are made of wood.

This gives a good view of the aircraft crane, which was made from a combination of wood, paper and photo-etch.

Below: The details of the back of the bridge and rebuilt searchlight tower, as well as the elaborate rigging, can be clearly seen in this picture.

Pierre kept on developing his scratch-building skills and in 1/500 there were lots of drawing available from the 'Ships Data Books' series; but 1/500 was still a bit small and in 1995 Pierre settled on 1/350 as his scale of choice.

Pierre has developed some unique modelling techniques to achieve the effects

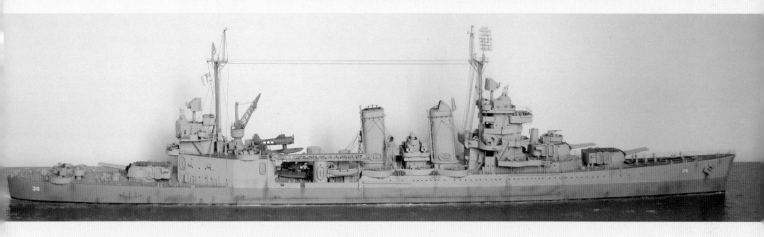

he requires. He uses paper where other builders use styrene; paper is thinner and more to scale. In this beautiful model Pierre used paper to make the cranes and details on vertical parts such doors and hatches; he even used rolled paper for barrels of the 8in guns. Pierre makes lots of his own photo-etch. The gunsights, platforms and other fine details on the 40mm mounts are an example of this, as are the 20mm. For the *Minneapolis* he developed a special set which included stack platforms, bollards, bottoms of life rafts, searchlight tower, cable reels and lifeboat davits.

For this model of the *Minneapolis* as she appeared after her final refit in 1945 all the principal parts of the ship, including hull, superstructure and turrets, are made of poplar wood. Many of the smaller items that are found in quantity on his models (such as lifeboats, searchlights, etc) are cast in resin by his friend Jacques Dreul of

Top: Pierre Marchal's model of the *Minneapolis* as she appeared in 1945.

Above: The photo-etch used for the searchlight tower was made specifically for this kit by Pierre.

The wake of the *Minneapolis* underway is beautifully done. One can easily imagine her steaming at a sedate 10 knots out of the anchorage.

With the port catapult removed in 1944 the whole hangar area opens up. This allows the modeller to show the workings of the scout aircraft. In this case they are Seamews, which came into service at the end of the war.

Below: This shows the *Minneapolis* serenely underway in a light harbour sea – the water is used to create this impression.

Bottom: The details of the final configuration of the *Minneapolis*'s superstructure are beautifully represented in this model. It is different from her sisters in that it is thinner. It is also shown after the large bridge windows were removed during her last refit.

L'Arsenal. For rigging Pierre uses a Canadian fishing thread designed for tying flies, employing two colours, brown and black, for effect. The standing rigging is black and the signal halyards are brown. The water is made with acrylic paint mixed with a gel to give it a luminous effect. When the 'sea' is dry he airbrushes with 'micro satin' to give it its sheen.

CLASSIC WARSHIPS *QUINCY* 1/350 SCALE

By KEN SUMMA

Left: This gives a view of the disinctive bridge supports of the *Quincy*. These supports were to be found only on the last two ships of the class, *Quincy* and *Vincennes*, as their bridge structure was different from the first five ships of the class.

Left, below: A full complement of scout planes on display. At this time the scout plane was the SOC Seagull, which served for most of the war on *New Orleans* class cruisers.

Below and bottom: Ken made this model of the *Quincy* for Steve Wiper, the proprietor of Classic Warships. This kit is now available through Yankee Modelworks.

Ken Summa is a well-known modeller who specialises in 1/700 but occasionally works at 1/350. Ken builds mainly in plastic but will do resin as well if the subject is interesting or the model is exceptional. He lives in Washington State and works in the defence industry. Ken built the Classic Warships *Quincy* out of the box and this shows just what can be done with the kit.

TRUMPETER *SAN FRANCISCO* 1/350 Scale

By PETE MARMANN

This lovely model of the *San Francisco* was built by Pete Marmann out of the Trumpeter kit. It shows the quality of the kit as well as Pete's building skills.

Like many modellers Pete became interested in ship model-making through the waterline 1/700 series of IJN ships first manufactured 40 years ago (and still going strong). They were inexpensive, all to the same scale and relatively easy to build. As a teenager Pete built a fleet of IJN subjects but his modelling lapsed as he assumed family and career responsibilities. Pete served for 24 years as a New York City Policeman – 'New York's Finest' as they are known. He was on duty on '9/11' 2001 but was not directly involved in rescue activities.

Now retired, Pete returned to his modelling interest, initially by building armour subjects, but then returned to his first interest – warships. Pete is also very interested in naval history, and particularly the Pacific War. One of the most famous ships from that era was the *San Francisco* – the most decorated cruiser of the war – and when, after 50 years of less-distinguished subjects, a plastic kit of this ship finally became available, Pete bought it and got to work immediately.

The build was pretty much out of the box, with accessories from Gold Metal Models photo-etch for the railings, radar,

Below: A view of the *San Francisco* as she would have appeared in 1942.

Bottom: The model was considerably enhanced by the addition of photo-etch from the Gold Medal Models 1/350 *San Francisco* set.

searchlight tower, etc, and L'Arsenal for the secondary and tertiary armaments. This model represents the *San Francisco* as she steamed into Ironbottom Sound on 12 November 1942, on the eve of the Battle of Guadalcanal.

The kit's Seagulls are quite nice. The panel lines are exaggerated close up but look good to the naked eye.

Below: The addition of L'Arsenal's 5in/25s gives a level of detail that cannot be achieved using the parts included in the kit.

SCRATCH-BUILT *SAN FRANCISCO* 1/192 Scale

By GARY KINGZETT

Gary Kingzett scratch-built this fine model of the *San Francisco* for Lou Parker, President of the USS *San Francisco* Crew Members Association. It is in 1/192 scale and shows the ship in her pre-war guise, with bare wood decks, squadron markings, and polished wood finishing on the boats – a very attractive subject.

When Gary was young he used to take his father's tools and saw a board into a rough shape of a destroyer hull. He found that sixpenny nails made an excellent 5in/38 barrel, and thus began a lifelong interest in modelling and especially scratch-building. When Gary could get his

hands on one, he would build models from Strombecker, a company noted for its wooden kits. He then moved on to the old Revell 'flat bottomed boats', the *Missouri*, the *Fletcher*, the *Helena* and others.

When Gary was 19 he found himself in San Francisco. At the time a private museum attached to Cliff House suffered fire damage. Gary offered to repair the forty or so ship models that were housed in the museum – he had no special qualifications but he was there and he made the offer. The opportunity to handle and repair so many high-quality models was a seminal experience. His own workmanship had to

San Francisco as she appeared in the pre-war period. This era provides some very interesting modelling subjects, as there were bits of colour and texture that were painted over during wartime. Note the squadron markings on the turrets and scout planes.

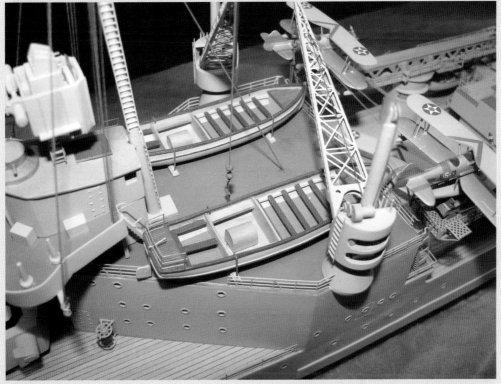

These ship's boats were made specifically for this model. The wood benches and gunwales give the model a touch of colour and texture in the hangar area.

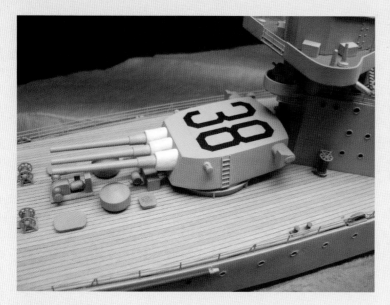

Above: Gary talked to men who had served aboard the ship during World War II. It made him feel good to be able to say, 'Art McArdle told me that *San Francisco*'s No 3 turret was painted chrome yellow for aerial recognition, so I painted it that way.'

Above, right: The different types of rigging can be seen, such as halyards, antennae and standing rigging like stays for mast and stack support.

Right: The wood deck was not painted over in peacetime. In this model the deck becomes quite a feature, adding surface texture. From the green stripe on the turret one can see that the *San Francisco* is in Squadron 7.

be the equal of the original professional model-builder. In repairing them he also had a chance to study building techniques and admire the craftsmanship of the original build.

Gary's modelling activities had to take a back seat as he moved East, started a family and a career as a design engineer for water treatment equipment. About ten years ago Gary got his hands on a Glencoe *Oregon* kit and the modelling itch returned. He built it up into a beautiful model that won best of class in the 1999 IPMS nationals. Since then he has won numerous prizes, including best ship in the IPMS 2005 Nationals.

The *San Francisco* model came about through a number of happy circumstances. Gary made the acquaintance of Lou Parker, President of the *San Francisco* Crew Members Association. Hearing of Lou and others' wartime experiences on this most decorated warship, Gary was moved to make a model of the ship and present it to Lou. This decision also brought it full circle to his time in San Francisco where he learned his craft and had studied the damaged bridge of the *San Francisco* placed near Cliff House as a memorial.

He made the *San Francisco* hull using

similar techniques to the building of the actual ship. He started with a framework and built the hull out of plastic sheets around the frame. The polystyrene sheets are .060in and .080in, the bottom sheet being the plan view of the waterline and a vertical sheet on the centreline forming the inboard profile. The length of the ship was divided into twenty-one hull stations, with a bulkhead at each shaped to the cross-

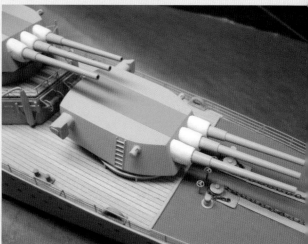

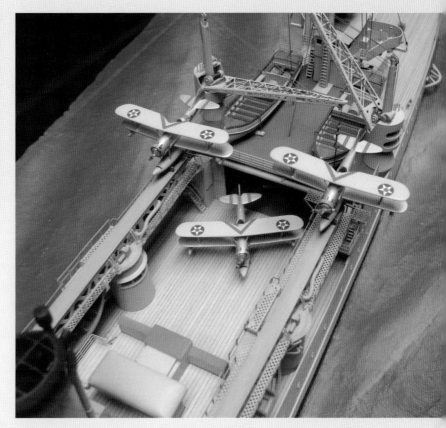

section of the hull at that point. Each hull side was formed from just one plastic sheet, the complex curves being formed by hot bending the side plate over a steam pipe. Where the curve proved too sharp, at the bow and stern, blocks of a cast urethane material called Butterboard were glued into place and carved to give the shape.

He made the 40ft launches from .020 vacuformed styrene. The masts are telescoping brass tubing and rod, tapered and soldered together. Solid structures were cut, turned, sanded or carved from Butterboard. Exposed decks and structures were fabricated from plastic sheet, from .005in to .020in. The wooden decks are pre-

glued sheet from Northeast Scale Products. Rope rigging was made from fishing line. To simulate steel cable, different grades of monofilament were used.

Although he scratch-built most of the ship's structure, Gary also made use of aftermarket parts. The 1/192 chocks and davits and the 26ft whaleboats are metal castings from Bluejacket, and he asked master modeller Don Preul to let him have some beautifully-cast 5in/25cal weapons from Don's own personal 1/192 arsenal. The jibs of the boat cranes and the catapults are photo-etch from Tom's Modelworks. The stanchions, railings, inclined ladders, cable reels and windlasses are from a generic 1:192 photo-etch set from Bluejacket.

Left: A view of the beautifully designed and cast 5in/25cal secondary armament from Don Preul's private 1/192 arsenal.

Above: Vought Corsair biplanes: they were painted with a silver fuselage and a bright chrome yellow on the wings. They also had a complex marking system to identify which squadron, ship and plane they were. These were shown in the letters on the side of the fuselage, paint pattern on the cowling, colour of the stripes on the rudder, and ailerons and the colour of the chevron on the wings.

This shows how the secondary armament was staggered, with the 5in in the middle set back from the ones fore and aft. This was true for all members of the class except the *Tuscaloosa*, where the weapon furthest aft was mounted inboard.

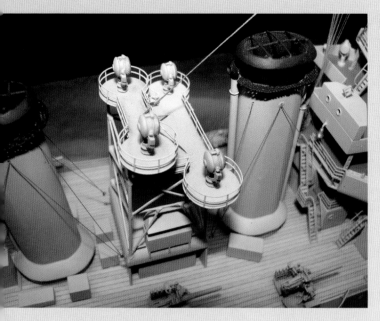

Above: The searchlight tower was built as a subassembly and installed on the wooden deck – just as in the real thing.

Above, right: A view of the beautifully designed and cast 5in/25cal secondary armament from Don Preul's private 1/192 arsenal.

Right: The signal halyards are nicely doubled up and connected to the flag bag. The halyard line is to scale and very realistic.

Gary says of his construction techniques:

I really do like building, making the shapes and subassemblies. I have never built a resin kit, primarily because it seems to me the kit builder had all the fun building the basic configuration, then making me do a whole bunch of fussy trimming and painting. It seems ridiculous to me to cast the tiny little deck machinery in place; it is difficult enough to paint a deck properly, and having to mask a whole bunch of tiny little parts makes it that much more difficult. Subassemblies let me do much more airbrush painting without masking. I dislike brush marks.

Gary uses a formula for lightening the dark colours to simulate looking through a long distance of moisture laden-atmosphere. The formula is to take the square root of the scale (e.g. 26 for 700, 18 for 350, 13 or 14 for 192), and add that much percentage of white or off-white to flat black. (for 1/700 26 parts white, 74 parts black). That sets the dark end of the spectrum. The formula does not work for the light colours, so for the light colours he blends in a bit of either a complementary or supplementary colour to get the full width of the visible palette.

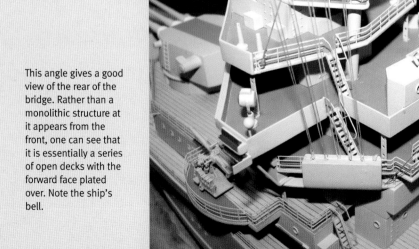

This angle gives a good view of the rear of the bridge. Rather than a monolithic structure at it appears from the front, one can see that it is essentially a series of open decks with the forward face plated over. Note the ship's bell.

NEW ORLEANS (MODIFIED TRUMPETER SAN FRANCISCO)
1/350 Scale

By DAVE HILL

Dave Hill is a very different type of modeller. He lives in an isolated rural community in Michigan, has never been to a model show (let alone enter a competition), has never met another experienced modelmaker in person – and yet he created this beautiful and accurate model of the *New Orleans* as she appeared in 1945.

Like many modellers Dave took up the hobby as a youngster. He built plastic kits out of the box – aircraft, armour, ships – the subject matter was not as important as the pleasure of making a good model. As Dave grew into his teens, he gravitated towards ships because he is a 'details' person and ship models have the greatest scope for adding detail. He also became very serious about his modelling at this time – he acquired an airbrush, started rigging his

models and adding what aftermarket components that were available at the time. However, other interests – women, work, wine – took him away from modelling for a period of fifteen years and the ship models of his childhood underwent a modelling Pearl Harbor.

When Dave was between jobs, he had lots of time on his hands and on impulse he bought a model of the *Gettysburg* by Dragon. Immediately he was hooked again and took his hobby to a new level of detail and workmanship. Working alone in the remote village of Kinde, Michigan, without direct reference to other modellers, Dave started to produce masterpiece after masterpiece. His most recent effort is this 1/350 model of the *New Orleans* as she appeared in 1945.

This model was adapted from the Trumpeter 1/350 *San Francisco* 1944 kit. Dave wanted to make a *New Orleans* because its war record was just as distinguished as the *San Francisco*'s but it seems to more neglected as a subject. He purchased some plans from Floating Drydock and commenced work, choosing to model the ship as it appeared in 1945 because he likes the look of 'late-war' ships. In order to convert the *San Francisco* kit he needed to do considerable scratch-building – particularly around the bridge and aft superstructure; there were significant differences between the two sisters after

Left, upper: The considerably reworked bridge area as it appeared in 1945.

Left, lower: Unlike the *Minneapolis*, SOC Seagulls served on the *New Orleans* until the end of the war.

Below: A model of the *New Orleans* as she appeared in 1945 – from the Trumpeter 1/350 *San Francisco* 1944 kit with significant scratch-building.

Right: This area had to be almost completely scratch-built as the configuration of the AA and superstructure was very different from the *San Francisco*.

Below: The aft 40mm quads were closer to the centreline and did not need sponsons like the *San Francisco* and *Minneapolis*.

several rebuilds and modernisations. Remarkably this was Dave's first attempt at scratch-building.

Dave represents a new phenomenon: he does network and correspond with other modelmakers; he does study other modellers' techniques and models, but he does it all online. Most other modellers of this standard have honed their skills by associating with others of similar interests, by attending and entering modelling competitions and by joining modelling clubs such as the local branch of the IPMS. Dave just does his modelling isolated in a small town in the thumb of Michigan and does not get around to modelling events or clubs or meetings. But he is a member of the modelling community, with a widespread network

of contacts, mentors and admirers – thanks to the internet.

In building this model Dave used lots of aftermarket parts and even mixed and matched them. For example, the 5in/25s are made from L'Arsenal barrels and Veteran models bases.

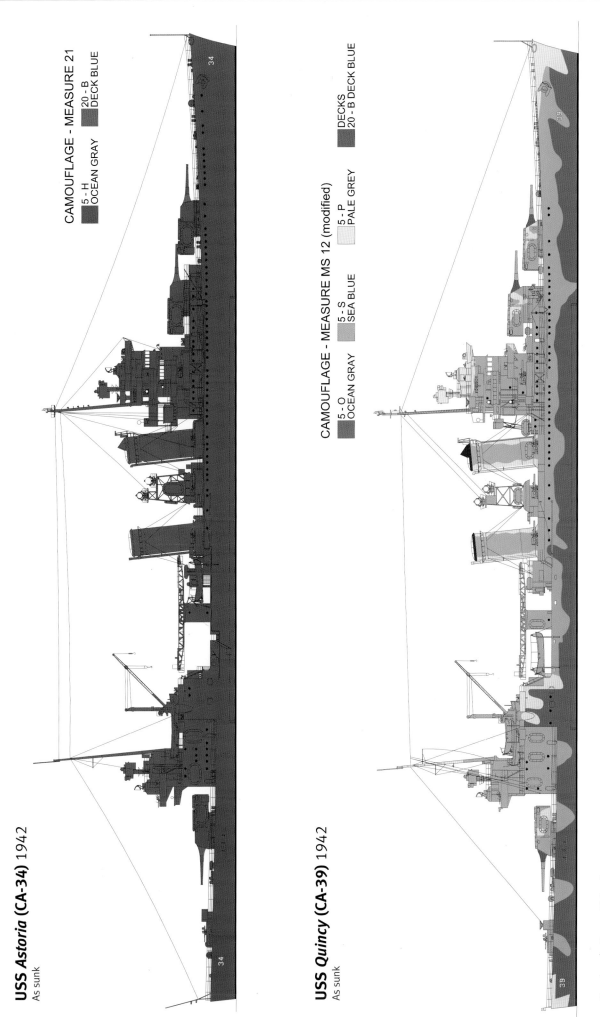

USS *Astoria* **(CA-34)** 1942
As sunk

CAMOUFLAGE - MEASURE 21

5 - H
OCEAN GRAY

20 - B
DECK BLUE

USS *Quincy* **(CA-39)** 1942
As sunk

CAMOUFLAGE - MEASURE MS 12 (modified)

5 - O
OCEAN GRAY

5 - S
SEA BLUE

5 - P
PALE GREY

DECKS
20 - B DECK BLUE

Drawings by George Richardson

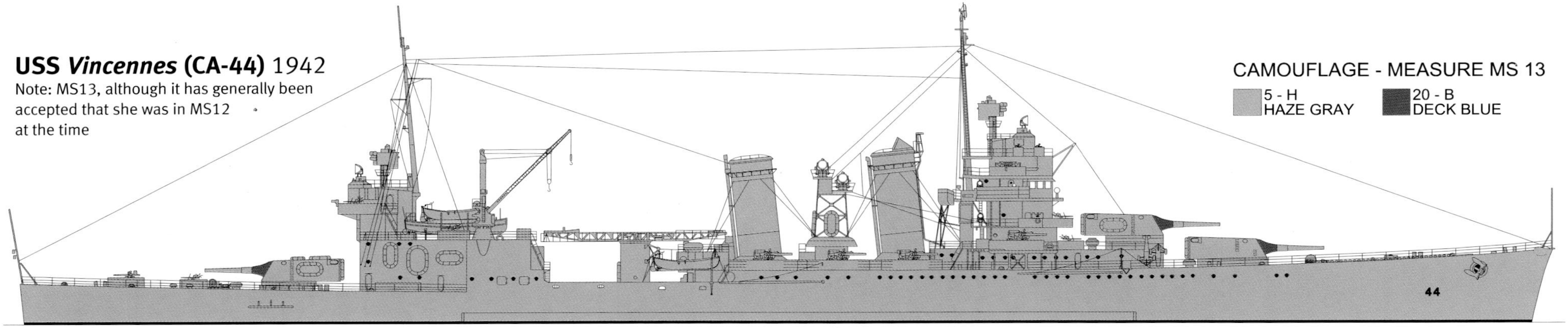

CAMOUFLAGE - MEASURE MS 13

5 - H
HAZE GRAY

20 - B
DECK BLUE

USS *Vincennes* (CA-44) 1942
Note: MS13, although it has generally been
accepted that she was in MS12
at the time

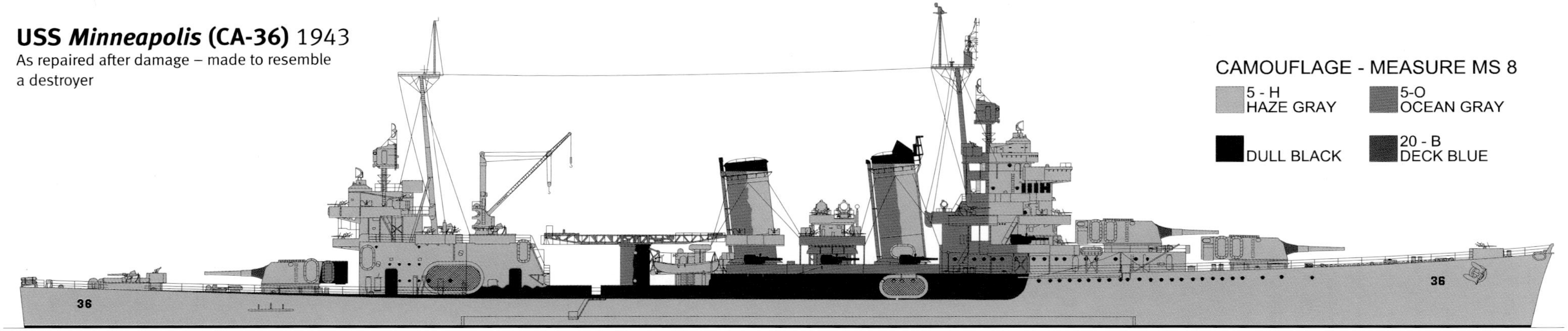

CAMOUFLAGE - MEASURE MS 8

5 - H
HAZE GRAY

5-O
OCEAN GRAY

20 - B
DECK BLUE

DULL BLACK

USS *Minneapolis* (CA-36) 1943
As repaired after damage – made to resemble
a destroyer

CAMOUFLAGE - MEASURE MS 22

5 - H
HAZE GRAY

5 - N
NAVY BLUE

20B
DECK BLUE

USS *Minneapolis* (CA-36) 1945
Typical end of war

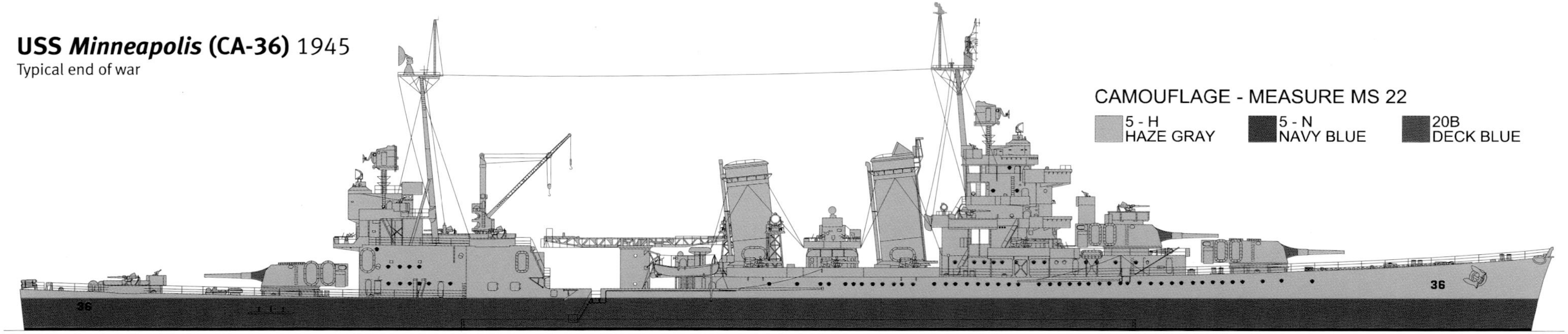

USS *San Francisco* (CA-38) 1944

CAMOUFLAGE - MEASURE MS 33 - 13D

5 - O
OCEAN GRAY

5 - L
LIGHT GRAY

20 - B
DECK BLUE

All drawings by George Richardson

Appearance

he *New Orleans* class formed three sub-classes in terms of appearance. The *New Orleans*, *Astoria* and *Minneapolis* had turrets with the front face of the 8in turrets rounded towards the top. The *San Francisco* and *Tuscaloosa* had a flat turret face and a newer model of 8in gun that was slightly thinner and allowed wider spacing of the muzzles. The last two of the class, the *Quincy* and *Vincennes*, had more significant differences in appearance. In order to reduce topweight and shorten the armour belt, the forward 8in turret was moved 9 feet aft. This meant that the forward deck-house had to be truncated, exposing the Number 2 turret's barbette. The bridge structure of these last two was different as well. The signal bridge was not as wide as the previous five ships in this class and supports for the bridge wings were required. The searchlight tower between the stacks was mounted atop the vent rather

than surrounding it. The stacks were also slightly thinner. The third pair of 5in guns were indented – but not as drastically as the previous five ships.

The *Tuscaloosa*, however, was an odd fish. Although nominally the same as the *San Francisco* she had one unique feature: the fourth pair of 5in were indented rather than the third pair as in all of the others in this class. Also the searchlight tower was mounted atop the vent – as in the *Vincennes* and *Quincy*. These differences were present when the ships were built, but as they were refitted just prior to the war and during the war, further distinctions arose.

Just before the war the signal bridges of the *Astoria*, *Minneapolis*, *San Francisco* and *Tuscaloosa* were plated in. The signal bridge was one and a half decks high and the windows were at full height in the *Astoria*, *Minneapolis* and *San Francisco* but only one deck high in the *Tuscaloosa*. The *New Orleans* never had her signal bridge plated

Opposite top: The *Minneapolis* refuelling at sea with Task Force 58 sometime in early 1944.

Opposite middle: The *Astoria* on manoeuvres just before the war.

Opposite bottom: A view of the *San Francisco*'s mainmast. Note the heavy braces and the platform on top. The secondary mast springing from the platform carries the SG surface search radar.

San Francisco. The signal bridge is plated in with windows at the top.

■ CLASS DIFFERENCES

Ship	Turret Face	Signal Bridge	Barbettes	5in Mountings
New Orleans	Rounded	Open	Closed	No 3 indented
Astoria	Rounded	Plated Up	Closed	No 3 indented
Minneapolis	Rounded	Plated Up	Closed	No 3 indented
San Francisco	Flat	Plated Up	Closed	No 3 indented
Tuscaloosa	Flat	Plated Down	Closed	No 4 indented
Vincennes	Flat	Open	Exposed	No 3 slightly Indented
Quincy	Flat	Open	Exposed	No 3 slightly Indented

Below, left: The searchlight tower of the *New Orleans* was similar to the ones on the *San Francisco*, *Astoria* and *Minneapolis* in that it straddled the vent.

Below, right: The tower on the *Quincy* sat atop the vent; this was also true for the *Vincennes* and *Tuscaloosa*.

in and the smaller bridge structure of *Quincy* and *Vincennes* did not lend itself to having the signal bridge plated in.

Splinter shields were fitted around the secondary armament in this period as well. The splinter shields were similar for all ships except the *Quincy*, where the shields had a simpler crescent shape and they were joined together. The other ships had a separate splinter shield for each mount.

The table above summarises the differences in the various ships in the class as at 1942.

PRE-WAR APPEARANCE

The pre-war appearance of the first five ships in this class were very sharp and elegant. They were painted a light grey and had colourful squadron markings on their turrets. These formed an interesting and eye-catching feature of these cruisers and were also applied to their scout planes. These squadron markings took the form of a broad stripe on turret No 2 and a large circle on turret No 3. The colour of the stripe indicated the squadron number and

the colour of the circle on the aft turret indicated the position within the squadron – the ship number. The flagship of the squadron was ship No 1.

The colours used on the second turret to designate squadron numbers were as follows:

Squadron 4 – Blue
Squadron 5 – Yellow
Squadron 6 – Black
Squadron 7 – Green

The number within the squadron, indicated by the circle on the aft turret was as follows: 1 = red, 2 = white, 3 = blue, 4 = black. This was called the Ship Colour. Therefore, the No 2 ship in Squadron 7 would be designated by a broad green stripe on the top of the second 8in turret and a large white disc painted on the top of the third turret.

Before the war the *New Orleans* cruisers served in Cruiser Squadrons 6 and 7. There was some movement between squadrons and within squadrons. For example, in July 1938 Cruiser Division 6 consisted of the *Minneapolis* (flagship and therefore ship No 1), *Astoria* ship No 2, *New Orleans* ship No 3 and the *Indianapolis* No 4; and Cruiser Division 7 had the *San Francisco* as flagship, *Quincy* No 2, *Vincennes* No 3 and *Tuscaloosa* No 4.

In 1940 the *San Francisco* moved to CruDiv 6 in the Pacific as Ship No 4 and the *Wichita* took over as Flagship of CruDiv 7 in the Atlantic, with the *Quincy* remaining as No 2. By December 1941 CruDiv 6 was unchanged in composition, but in CruDiv 7 (still in the Atlantic) the *Quincy* had become the flagship, *Tuscaloosa* No 2 and *Vincennes*

No 3. This system was discontinued after Pearl Harbor, but the stripes and discs stayed on until the ship was next serviced and painted. In some cases the designations stayed on as late as mid-1942, but this will help any modeller who wants to get the squadron and ship markings correct.

The seaplanes carried by these ships add interest and in their pre-war guise a dash of colour. These cruisers could carry up to four scout seaplanes and that was their normal complement. Initially they carried Vought Corsair biplanes that were replaced in 1939 by SOC Seagulls, which were also biplanes. They were painted with a silver fuselage and a bright chrome yellow on the wings. They also had a complex marking system to identify which squadron, ship and plane they were. These were shown in the letters on the side of the fuselage. Each plane had the following sequence [Division]-CS-[plane number].

The division number was the same as the cruiser's division number. CS appeared on all scout planes – it stood for Cruiser Scout. The plane number was not so straightforward: each cruiser had up to four planes so the plane numbers of the flagship in the division were 1, 2, 3 and 4; ship No 2 in the division had plane numbers 5-8, ship No 3 had plane numbers 9-12, and so forth.

The rudder of each plane had a single horizontal stripe which was painted the division colour. Atop the upper wing there was a chevron painted the ship colour, as was the cowling. To further complicate things the cowling was painted in different patterns depending on which plane number it was. Plane No 1 had the entire cowling painted in the ship colour; No 2 had the upper half painted in the ship colour while the lower half remained silver; No 3 had the lower half of the cowling painted; and plane No 4 had a broad horizontal stripe on each side of the cowling painted in the ship colour. Just to make sure of things, the ailerons of each plane had a single broad stripe running fore and aft painted ship colour.

For example: in 1939 the *Vincennes* was ship No 3 in Cruiser Division 7. Therefore its division colour was green and its ship colour was blue. Plane No 2 of the *Vincennes* in 1939 would have the designation 7-SC-10 on each side, a blue chevron painted on the top wing, a green horizontal stripe on the

rudder, the lower half of the cowling painted blue and a blue stripe on the aileron. It would look good on any model.

This all changed by mid-1941 when all the aircraft were painted grey and the markings were painted out, leaving only the fuselage numbers.

PRE-WAR MODIFICATIONS

With the war in Europe intensifying and tension with Japan increasing, the seven *New Orleans* class cruisers were taken in hand and prepared for war. They were painted either in Navy Blue or a camouflage scheme. Splinter shields were put around the 5in secondary armament and four quad 1.1in anti-aircraft mounts were installed – two on the fantail and two above the navigation bridge. Additional anti-aircraft armament in the form of eight single 20mm Oerlikons were installed as well. These were located on the same deck as, and just aft of, No 2 turret, atop the hangar deck just aft of the cranes, and a gallery of four of them surrounding the aft control station.

With the exception of the splinter shields and paint jobs the ships had much the

The *Quincy* and *Vincennes* had lighter bridges with fewer windows. They also had an open signal bridge.

The *San Francisco* is ready for war. The 5in guns have splinter shields protecting them from spray and shrapnel, she has been painted in Measure 21 camouflage – Navy Blue on all vertical surfaces – and one can clearly see the gallery of 20mm AA surrounding the aft fire control station.

Above: The *New Orleans* dockside refitting. Note the 20mm platform from the chopped-down searchlight tower to the aft stack. Also note the position of the forward 40mm gun tub.

Below: The after section of the *New Orleans* dockside refitting. Note the positions of the 40mm guns tub atop the hangar. There is no port catapult and there is no overhang of the 40mm gun tubs on the fantail.

same shape and form as their pre-war appearance until late 1942 when three were sunk and three more badly damaged. While the damage was being repaired, an opportunity was taken to do a major refit of the superstructure and light AA armament. These modifications considerably altered the ships' appearance.

MID-WAR RECONSTRUCTION

The role of cruisers changed during the war, shifting from surface warfare to shore bombardment and screening the fast carrier forces. The remaining cruisers had their AA armament dramatically increased. Their superstructures were rebuilt to a more compact profile so that the increased AA could have better arcs of fire and to counterbalance the increased topweight that these new weapons engendered.

In the interest of less topweight they also lost their starboard crane. The *Minneapolis* and *New Orleans* lost their port catapult later in the war as well, which demonstrates that there was less emphasis on the scouting role of cruisers. Instead of scout plane facilities they received 40mm quads above the hangar. There were also 40mm quads replacing the 1.1in on the fantail and a deck lower on the bridge.

The position of the quad mounts differed on the various ships. In the *San Francisco*, *Tuscaloosa* and *Minneapolis* the gun tubs on top of the hangar were staggered – on the

starboard side the gun tub was where the crane had been, and the port gun tub was well behind the position of the remaining crane. The *Tuscaloosa*'s starboard mount was located farther aft than the other two. On the *New Orleans* the port gun tub was in the same location, but the starboard one was abreast the portside one. Also, in the *New Orleans* the fantail quads were mounted closer to the centreline, whereas the other three ships required sponsons to support the tub. The forward quads were mounted just aft and a deck higher than the first 5in/25 weapon.

There was also a massive increase in the number of 20mm from twelve to twenty-six. Ten of these extra 20mm were mounted around the now truncated searchlight tower and a platform around the aft stack. The *New Orleans* and *Tuscaloosa* had a continuous platform from the tower to the middle of the aft stack, whereas the other two had a platform around the stack and four more positions on the tower itself.

The splinter shields around the secondary armament were also altered so that they all joined together rather than each weapon having its own shield. This was similar to the *Quincy* but the shields are more irregularly shaped. The *Tuscaloosa* had a different arrangement because the 5in guns were themselves disposed differently.

The most dramatic change was in the bridge. In all four surviving ships it was

Above: The *San Francisco*'s splinter shields were typical of the other cruisers where each 5in mounting had its own enclosure.

Above, left: The *Quincy*'s splinter shields were different from the others. They were a simple crescent shape and joined together.

completely rebuilt to allow better arcs of fire and better control of the type of action that the ships were likely to be involved in. They now had a blocky monolithic appearance and a large open bridge atop the battle bridge forward and just below the Mk 33 director. However, all four cruisers showed detail differences.

The *San Francisco* emerged from the yards with a solid four and a half storey structure surmounted by a large overhanging open bridge. The conning tower remained in front of the signal bridge, and there was a small gallery in front of the conning tower. The structure extended aft of the old signal bridge, extending as far aft as the new pole foremast. The *Tuscaloosa* was similarly rebuilt but with a larger gallery with four 20mm around the conning tower.

The *Minneapolis*, however, was significantly different. The tower structure was the same height but it was much narrower. The rear of the bridge structure was 10ft forward of the foremast and the battle bridge had distinctive large windows. The *New Orleans* had its new bridge structure built atop the signal bridge deckhouse and conning tower. There was a lot of open space behind No 2 turret. Also the open bridge atop the structure remained unsheltered all the way to the mast.

In all four ships thick modern polemasts replaced the previous foremast and mainmast. There was a platform atop each mast for supporting all of the new radar and elec-

tronic equipment. The foremast platform supported the SK-2 radar and a small mast for mounting the SG surface radar. In the *Tuscaloosa*, *San Francisco* and *New Orleans* the foremast was directly abaft the bridge structure whereas in the *Minneapolis* it was about 10ft abaft the bridge structure.

CAMOUFLAGE SCHEMES

This class of ships carried a variety of differing camouflage schemes during the war years. At the end of the war all of the surviving members of the class were wearing Measure 22 – Navy Blue below the sheer line and Haze Gray above. Prior to that there was a mixture – but not as varied as some of the other classes. For instance the *New Orleans* was painted in Measure 21 – Navy Blue on all horizontal surfaces – almost all of the war. Early in the war the *Tuscaloosa*, *Quincy* and *Vincennes* wore a Measure 13 'splotch' camouflage. Indeed that was how the *Quincy* and *Vincennes* were painted when they met their demise. In 1943 the *Minneapolis* wore a unique Measure 8 camouflage that was intended to make her resemble a *Benson* class destroyer. Only the *Tuscaloosa* and *San Francisco* ever wore a 'splinter' scheme and it was the same one – Ms 33/13d, a scheme designed for destroyers. Ms 33 was the lighest of the three splinter schemes and used combinations of Ocean Grey, Haze Gray and Light Gray for their pattern.

Below: The *San Francisco* in Measure 33/13d. This scheme was designed for destroyers and indeed was on a number of famous destroyers during the war.

Bottom: the starboard view of *San Francicso* Measure 33/13d.

■ CAMOUFLAGE MEASURES

Name	1942	1943	1944	1945
New Orleans	Ms 21	Ms 21	Ms 21	Ms 22
Astoria	Ms 21	–	–	–
Minneapolis	Ms 21	Ms 8	Ms 21	Ms 22
San Francisco	Ms 21	Ms 21	Ms 33 13d	Ms 22
Tuscaloosa	Ms 12 Mod	Ms 22	Ms 33 13d	Ms 22
Quincy	Ms 12 Mod	–	–	–
Vincennes	Ms 12 Mod	–	–	–

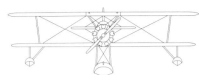

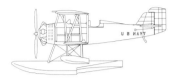

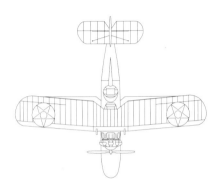

The *Tuscaloosa* retained individual splinter shields for each 5in/25. Note the 20mm gallery attached to the bridge – this was also unique to the *Tuscaloosa*.

Vought O2U-1 Corsair

Above: A <u>very</u> rare glimpse of the camouflaged port side of the *Vincennes*. This is the only photo this author has been able to find of it.

Below: The starboard side is well photographed. The colours are the same as the *Quincy*'s.

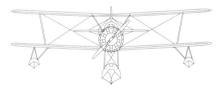

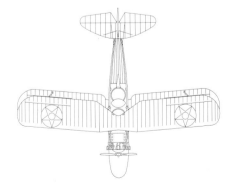

Vought O3U-1 Corsair

Drawings by George Richardson

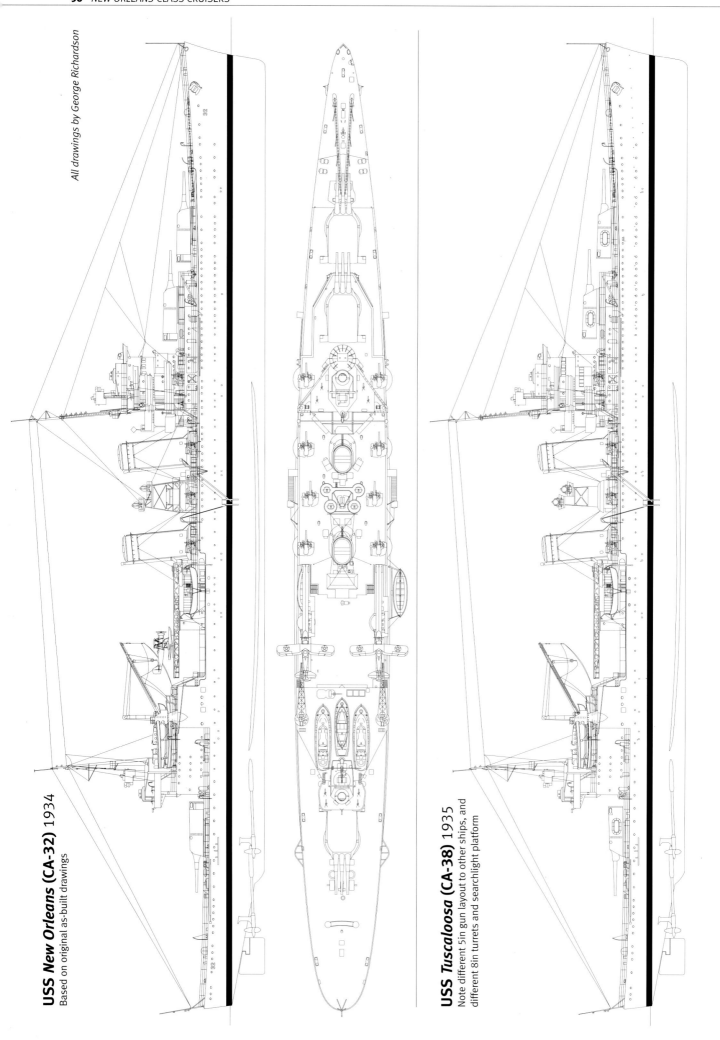

All drawings by George Richardson

USS *New Orleans* (CA-32) 1934
Based on original as-built drawings

USS *Tuscaloosa* (CA-38) 1935
Note different 5in gun layout to other ships, and different 8in turrets and searchlight platform

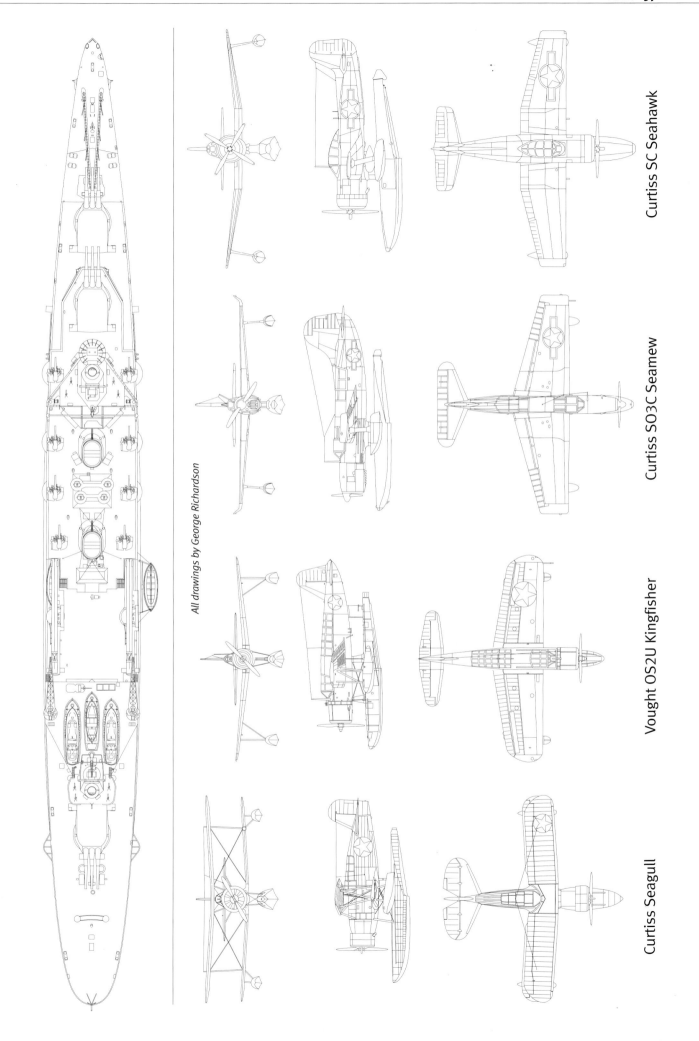

All drawings by George Richardson

Curtiss SC Seahawk

Curtiss SO3C Seamew

Vought OS2U Kingfisher

Curtiss Seagull

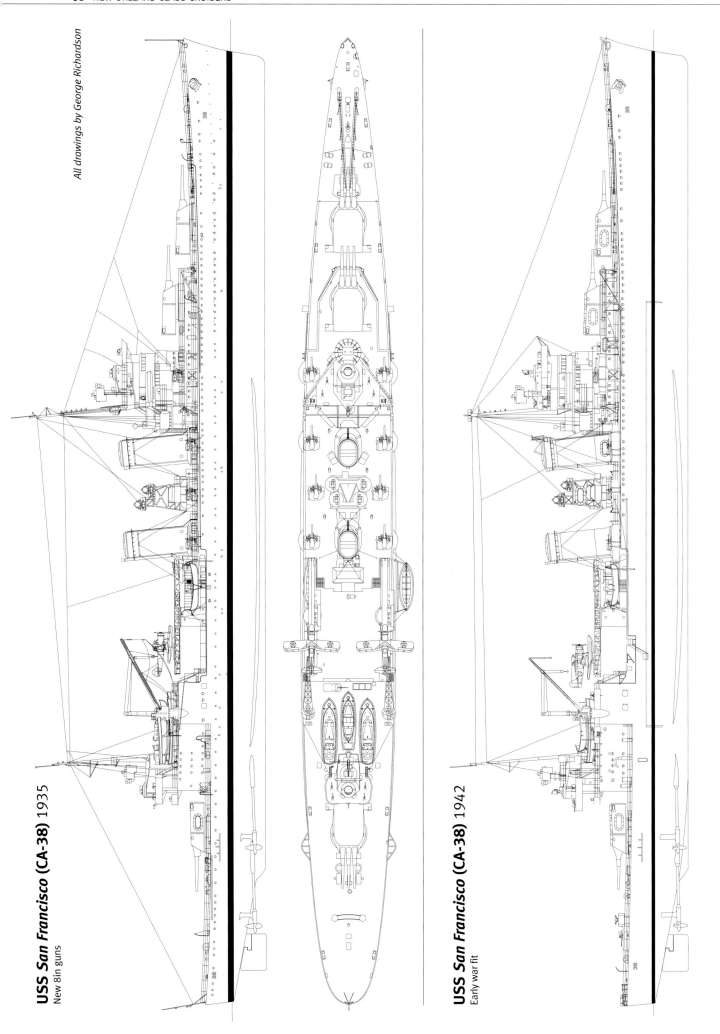

All drawings by George Richardson

USS *San Francisco* (CA-38) 1935
New 8in guns

USS *San Francisco* (CA-38) 1942
Early war fit

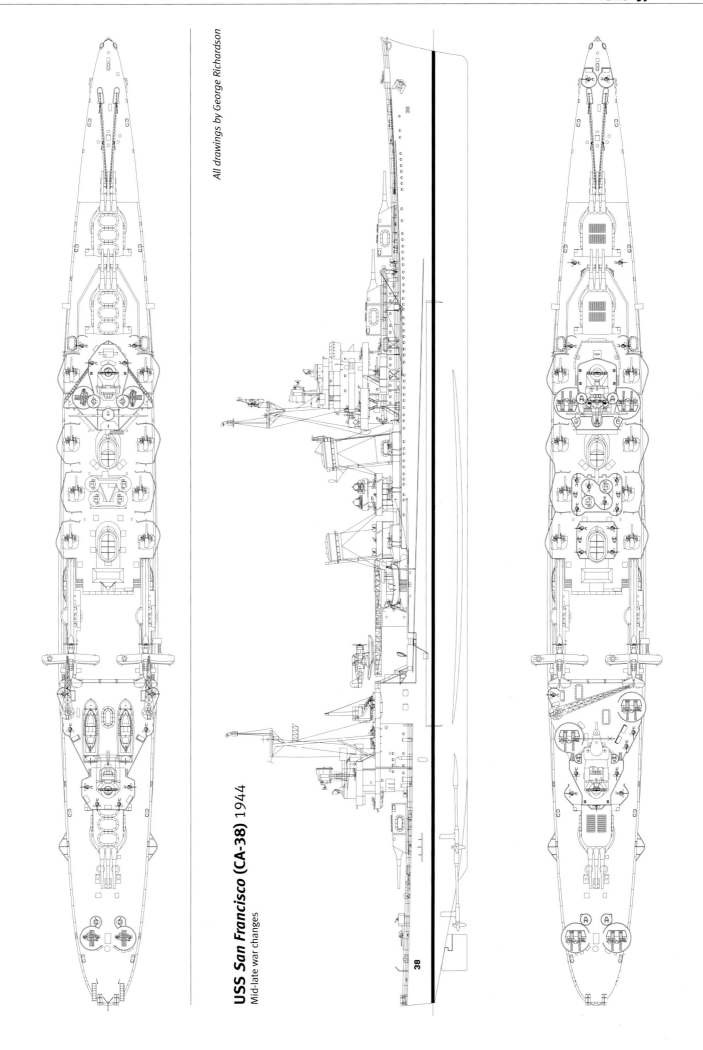

All drawings by George Richardson

USS *San Francisco* (CA-38) 1944
Mid-late war changes

All drawings by George Richardson

USS Minneapolis (CA-36) 1942
Early war fit

USS Minneapolis (CA-36) 1943
As repaired after serious damage

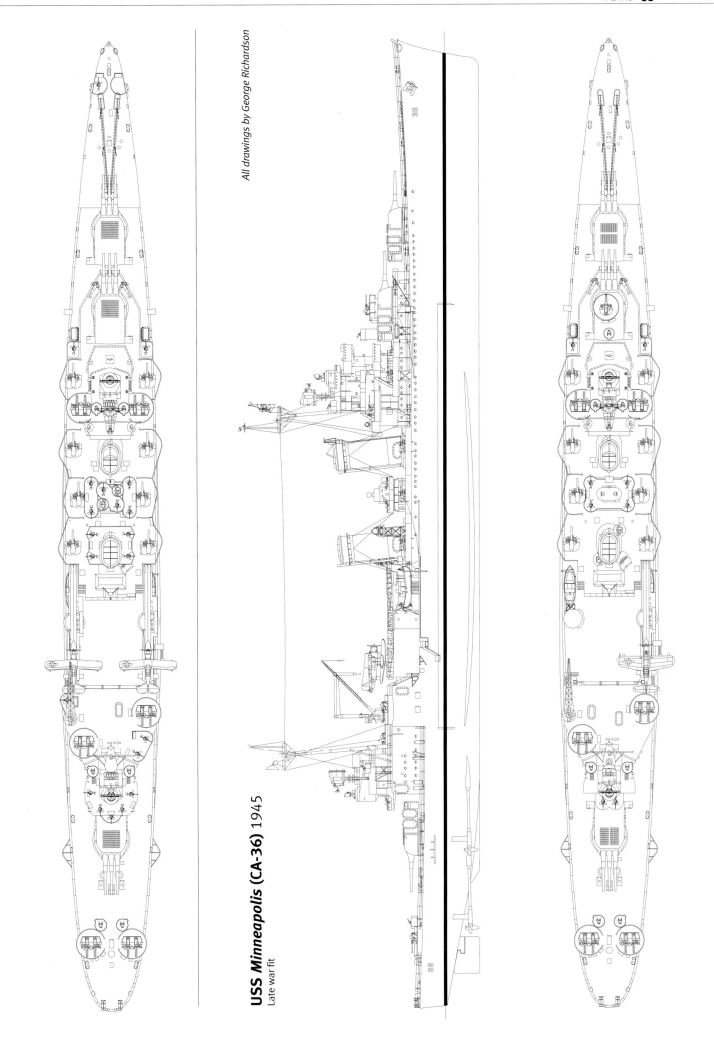

All drawings by George Richardson

USS *Minneapolis* (CA-36) 1945
Late war fit

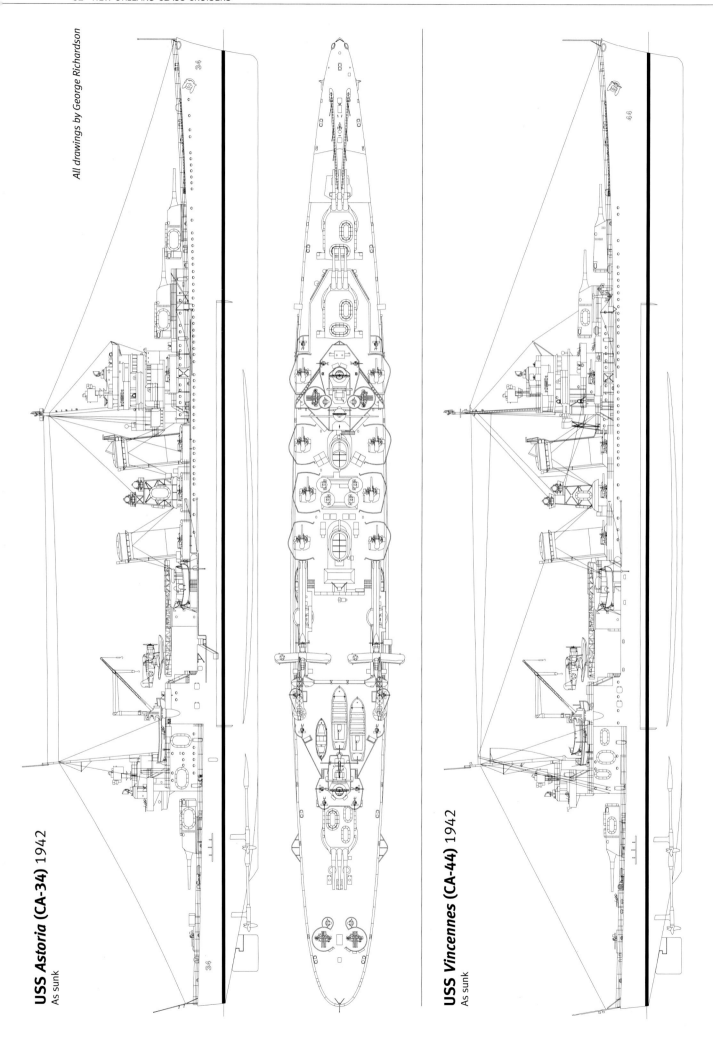

All drawings by George Richardson

USS *Astoria* **(CA-34)** 1942
As sunk

USS *Vincennes* **(CA-44)** 1942
As sunk

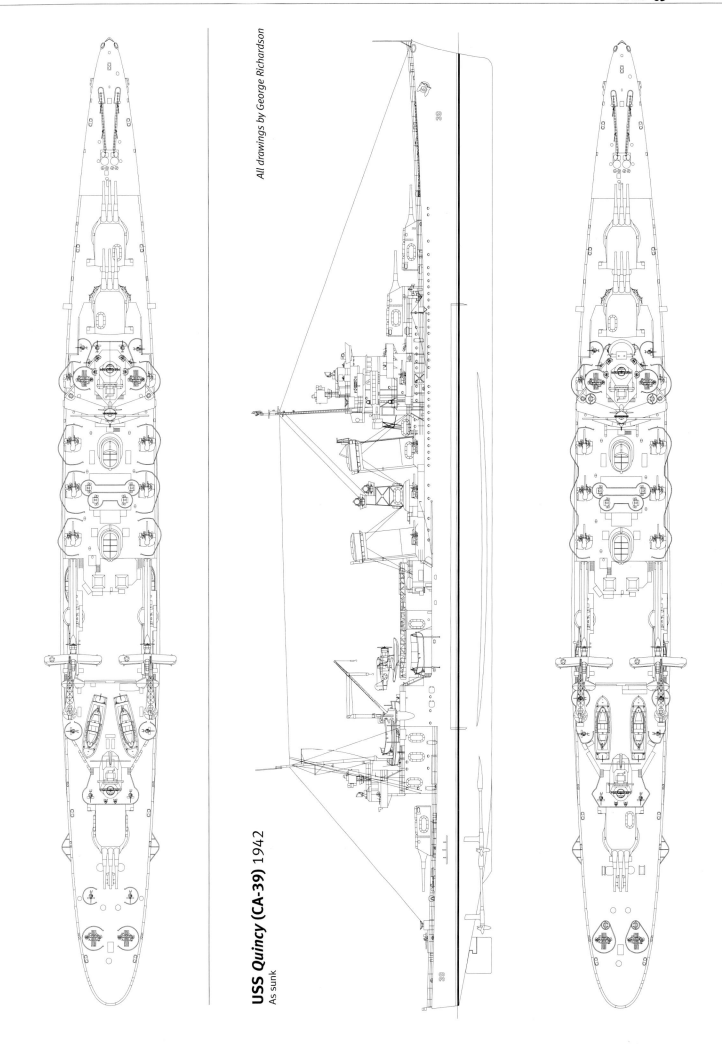

All drawings by George Richardson

USS *Quincy* **(CA-39)** 1942
As sunk

Selected References

BOOKS

Adcock, Al, *Heavy Cruisers in Action Part 1,* Squadron Signal Publications (Carrollton 2001).

Cutler, Thomas J, *The Battle of Leyte Gulf,* Harper Collins (New York 1994)

Ewing, Steve, *American Cruisers of World War II,* Pictorial Histories Publishing Company (Missoula 1984).

Friedman, Norman, *US Cruisers: An Illustrated Design History,* Naval Institute Press (Annapolis 1985).

Grace, James W, *The Naval Battle of Guadalcanal, Night Action 13 November 1942,* Naval Institute Press (Annapolis 1999).

Morison, Samuel Eliot, *History of US Naval Operations in WWII:* Vols *V The Struggle for Guadalcanal; VI Breaking the Bismarcks Barrier; VII Aleutians, Gilberts and Marshalls; VIII New Guinea and the Marianas; XII Leyte; XIII Liberation of the Philippines; XIV Victory in the Pacific; XV Supplement and General Index,* Little Brown and Co. (Boston 1951-1960).

Stern, Robert, *US Navy 1942-1943,* Arms and Armour Press (London 1990).

US Naval Vessels 1943, Naval Institute Press and Arms and Armour Press, Annapolis and London 1986). Originally published in 1943 as ONI-54 series.

Walkowiak, Thomas & Sowinski, Larry, *United States Navy Camouflage of the WW2 Era Part 1,* The Floating Drydock (Kresgeville 1976, 1988).

Wiper, Steve, *Warship Pictorial #2: Minneapolis CA-36,* Classic Warships Publications (Tucson 1997).

Wiper, Steve, *Warship Pictorial #5: San Francisco CA-38,* Classic Warships Publications (Tucson 1999).

Wiper Steve, *Warship Pictorial #7 New Orleans Class Cruisers,* Classic Warships Publications (Tucson 2000).

WARSHIP MODELLING WEBSITES

www.modelwarships.com
www.smmlonline.com
www.steelnavy.com
www.ipmsusa.com
www.warshipmodelsunderway.com

WARSHIP RESEARCH WEBSITES

www.historycentral.com/NAVY/cruiser
www.shipcamouflage.com/warship_camouflage.htm
www.navsource.org
www.history.navy.mil
www.classicwarships.com
www.hazegray.org

ACKNOWLEDGEMENTS

Steve Wiper
Ken Hoolihan
Loren Perry
White Ensign Models
Hunter Abbey
Elizabeth Abbey

The *Quincy* had a three-colour scheme using Navy Blue, Ocean Gray and Haze Gray.